HELPING YOUR UNDERACHIEVER

BECOME A SUCCESSFUL STUDENT

The
Unmotivated
Child

Natalie Rathvon, Ph.D.

A Fireside Book

PUBLISHED BY SIMON AND SCHUSTER

FIRESIDE
Rockefeller Center
1230 Avenue of the Americas
New York, NY 10020

FIRESIDE and colophon are registered
trademarks of Simon & Schuster Inc.

Designed by Jennifer Ann Daddio

Manufactured in the United States of America

5   7   9   10   8   6   4

Library of Congress Cataloging-in-Publication Data is available.

ISBN 0-684-80306-2

To my husband, James——my own secure base

. . . a thing which has not been understood inevitably reappears; like an unlaid ghost, it cannot rest until the mystery has been solved and the spell broken.

SIGMUND FREUD, 1909

Contents

Part Three:
Pathways to Achievement

Introduction:

The Mystery of Underachievement

John and his parents are sitting at the dining room table. His father looks angry, his mother looks worried, and John looks discouraged. His father holds John's report card in his hand.

"Son, how can anybody with your intelligence make four Ds and two Fs?" his father asks. "Your teachers say you're not turning in most of your homework. And you didn't hand in a project in science or social studies."

Wringing her hands, his mother exclaims, "John, why don't you do your work? You know you can do it! And you know we'll help you if you need it." John slumps down in his chair and looks forlornly at the floor.

"John, answer your mother when she's talking to you!" his father snaps. "Why aren't you doing your schoolwork?"

"I don't know," John mumbles.

His father shakes his head disgustedly. "Son, you've got to work harder. From now on, when you get home from school, I want you to go up to your room and I don't want you to come down until that homework is done."

"OK, Dad. I'll try harder," promises John.

This scene is played out in thousands of households across the country between parents and underachieving children. The parents feel frustrated because they don't understand why their bright child isn't doing his work. They feel anxious about his educational and career prospects, and they feel angry that he doesn't work harder in school. They are even more frustrated because he can't seem to come up with an explanation of *why* he isn't doing his work.

For his part, the child feels discouraged about his poor grades and his inability to solve his problems. He knows he has disappointed his parents, and he is deeply disappointed in himself. But he is telling the truth when he says that he doesn't know why he doesn't do his work. And although his parents have accurately pointed out what he needs to do (work harder), and he genuinely wants to do better to please his parents and to feel better about himself, he will almost certainly fail to keep his promise to improve.

For some unfortunate children, underachievement seems almost inevitable, or at least understandable. Children living in impoverished environments grow up in an atmosphere permeated with hopelessness and helplessness. It is not surprising that many of these children, trapped within the vicious cycle of poverty and despair, have trouble succeeding in school. But many underachievers do not come from families beset by cultural and economic deprivation. Like John, they come from families that are able to provide the resources that support academic achievement. They are bright, even gifted youngsters who don't do their work or who consistently perform at a level below their ability. Their underachievement is a mystery—to their parents, their teachers, and themselves.

If parents focus their attention only on the child's current school situation, they will not be able to understand why he isn't performing better. There is no good reason why John, with all his ability, can't do his work—or rather, there is no good *rational* reason. But the key to the mystery of underachievement does not lie in rational processes or even in conscious processes. The key lies beneath the surface behavior—that is, the child's failure to perform—in the internal set of beliefs that guide his attitudes and actions.

NEW PERSPECTIVES ON AN OLD PROBLEM

The view of underachievement presented here is based on attachment theory, which is an outgrowth of the psychoanalytic theory developed by Sigmund Freud. It also draws on research in developmental psychology, learning and motivation theory, and my own years of working with underachievers and their families. Attachment theorists, such as John Bowlby and Mary Ainsworth, propose that all human beings are motivated to form close emotional bonds, or *attachments*, with other human beings throughout their lives, and that our capacity to form attachments has a great deal to do with our ability to function effectively in the world. People who have secure, loving attachments are able to accept and give help to others, develop satisfying relationships, and pursue their goals with confidence and enthusiasm. In contrast, those who have difficulty forming secure attachments develop a distrust of their own worth and competence and the willingness of others to help them meet their needs. Such insecurely attached individuals are plagued with chronic feelings of emptiness, dissatisfaction, and anxiety. They are unable either to reach their maximum potential or to develop and maintain fulfilling relationships with others.

According to attachment theory, the ability to form attachments is primarily based on the nature of the interactions children have with their parents and other caretakers during infancy and childhood. For children to develop secure attachments, they must be able to satisfy two basic needs. First, they must feel safe and cared for, and second, they must feel supported and validated in their efforts to explore their world. When children are fortunate enough to have reasonably warm, consistent, and supportive parenting, they have what we call a *secure base*—a sanctuary where they can meet their dual needs for nurturance and validation. Such children internalize an image of themselves as lovable and competent and an image of others as responsive and helpful. As a result, they have a secure base not only in the external environment in the form of their parents but also within themselves to comfort and encourage them wherever they go. Attachment theorists refer to these mental representations of the self and others as *working models*, indicating that the person's internal images are continually undergoing modi-

fications and adjustments, especially in the early stages of their formation.

But for some children, finding a secure base is not so easy. Many parents today were unable to obtain the kind of security and validation
they needed as children from their own families. When they come to
parenthood, their lack of a secure base during their own development,
lack of support from others in their present lives, or both make it hard
for them to provide their children with the kind of consistent encouragement that builds positive working models of the self and others.
Other youngsters have such overwhelming developmental problems
that they tax the physical and emotional resources of even the most
supportive parents. In either case, such children internalize an image of
themselves as somehow unlovable and incompetent and an image of
others as unavailable and unhelpful. They have trouble feeling secure
either in the outside world or within themselves.

When the child comes to school, she brings with her these internal
views of herself and others, and they guide her interactions with teachers and peers. In fact, she tends to behave in ways that induce those
around her to behave as her internal world tells her to expect. The
child with a secure base is cheerful, eager to learn, and easily soothed
when frustrated. As a result, she receives positive responses from teachers and peers that build feelings of self-esteem and motivate her to persist with challenging tasks. But the child whose base is not so secure
expects that others will be unhelpful, critical, and rejecting. Unconsciously she sets up situations in which she evokes those responses from
others. And with every negative response, her internal belief that she is
unlovable and incompetent is reinforced. So begins the vicious cycle of
underachievement, as the child's maladaptive beliefs lead to ineffective
behaviors, followed by negative reactions from parents, teachers, and
peers that reinforce her distorted internal perspective and further erode
positive feelings about the self and its capacity to master developmental
tasks.

I want to emphasize here that it is not the intent of this book to
blame parents. Years of working with parents have taught me that all
parents do the very best they can with their children, given their ability
to obtain support and encouragement for parenting. Moreover, the as-

signing of blame that occurs so often with the underachiever is counterproductive, because it prevents the underachiever and the people
trying to help her from relying on each other for support. Rather, this
book is intended to alert parents to the need to identify and alter ineffective interactional patterns that inhibit their child's academic
progress. No parents wish their child to be an underachiever, any more
than any child wishes to be a school failure. Unfortunately, however,
ineffective interactional patterns tend to be passed down from one generation to the next, so that the best-intentioned parents often perpetuate the same inappropriate ways of relating to and communicating with
their children that their parents used with them.

At the same time, however, this approach also stresses that parents
are the most powerful change agents in the process of treating the underachiever. By modifying the way in which they interact with him,
they can help him modify the inappropriate internal beliefs that give
rise to underachievement. Throughout the treatment process, the focus
is on communication. Parents are helped to understand the messages
the underachiever is trying to convey through his bewildering and frustrating behaviors and to communicate more constructively with him.
Because a person's view of himself and others is shaped to a great extent
by the way in which others talk to him and talk about him in the presence of others, this approach stresses identifying and practicing ways of
communicating that enhance the underachiever's feelings of self-worth
and encourage his investment in his educational experiences. Parents
are also helped to communicate more effectively with the other significant adults in the child's learning environment—his teachers—so that
they, too, can more effectively support his efforts to achieve.

This book is organized in three parts. Part One describes the pathways
to underachievement. Chapter 1, "The Road to Underachievement,"
describes the warning signs of underachievement in elementary, middle,
and high school and traces the insidious progression of the undetected
and untreated syndrome. Chapter 2, "Identifying the Underachiever,"
helps parents learn to distinguish underachievement from other problems, such as the boredom of the gifted student, learning disabilities,
and Attention-Deficit/Hyperactivity Disorder, and learn how to collab-

orate with teachers to obtain an accurate assessment of the child's academic and social problems. In Part Two, parents are taken on a journey into the underachiever's mysterious world. Chapter 3 describes the underachiever's internal world, with the irrational beliefs underlying his baffling behaviors that sabotage his ability to succeed and drive parents and teachers to distraction. In Chapter 4, the profoundly negative effects of that internal world on the underachiever's school experiences are revealed, including not only his classroom performance but also his relationships with teachers and classmates. Four styles of underachiever behavior are described, all of which derive from the maladaptive internal perspective described earlier.

Part Three is devoted to the practical program of treating the underachiever. Chapter 5, "The Problem with the Solution: Why Treatments Fail," describes common interventions for underachievement and helps parents understand why they don't and can't work, thus saving precious time in the treatment process. Chapter 6, which forms the heart of the treatment program, opens the door to change by helping parents communicate constructively rather than destructively with the underachiever. Parents first learn how to translate the underachiever's frustrating and incomprehensible way of expressing himself and then learn five constructive communication strategies that help the underachiever modify his ineffective views of himself and others so that he can approach his school tasks with confidence and enthusiasm. Chapter 7, "The Homework Trap and How to Get Out of It," offers seven practical strategies on all aspects of helping the underachiever manage his homework effectively, ranging from how to get him started on his homework to how to help him get it back to school. Although parents may think that there is little they can do to influence their child's behavior in the classroom, this is certainly not the case! Chapter 8, "Teaming with Teachers," describes eight practical techniques that encourage teachers' assistance and commitment to the treatment process and help the underachiever develop more effective behaviors in the classroom. Because the underachiever very often presents behavior problems as well as academic problems, Chapter 9 provides parents with insight into the message hidden behind the underachiever's misbehavior and offers strategies for helping him manage his negative feelings more productively. Finally, Chapter 10, "The Transformation Process," describes how change occurs and provides guidelines for supporting the underachiever, his teachers, and other family members through the change process and dealing constructively with the inevitable setbacks on the road to recovery. Trying to understand and help the underachiever can be frustrating, but it can also be a deeply rewarding experience for parents as they learn and change together with their child.

Part One

Pathways
to
Underachievement

I.

The Road to Underachievement

Danny is an attractive seven-year-old second grader who lives with his parents and four-year-old sister in a middle-class neighborhood with excellent schools. Although he seems bright and has a good vocabulary, he completes very little written work in school. Instead, he spends his time playing with toys he has smuggled into class, fidgeting restlessly in his chair, or just gazing into space. Danny's teacher tells his parents that she has tried everything to get him to do his work. His frantic parents are beside themselves with worry. They remind each other of how much Danny enjoyed preschool and kindergarten. His first-grade teacher did say he was "immature," but she assured them he'd grow out of it. They can't understand what has gone wrong or what to do about it.

Sam is a stocky thirteen-year-old seventh-grade youngster with an IQ of 135. Despite his ability, he has done poorly in school since fourth grade. Retained in sixth grade because he failed to turn in most of his homework, Sam is in danger of failing again. Since entering middle school, he has become the class clown, constantly trying to amuse his classmates and avoiding his academic work. After his last report card (three Cs, two Ds, and an F), his parents grounded him for two weeks and ordered him to write down his assignments in a notebook and have his teachers sign it every day. After three days, Sam forgot to ask his teachers to sign his notebook. After a week, he lost the notebook. Sam's

father is so angry that he is threatening to send him to a military board-
ing school 150 miles away.

A petite, pretty tenth-grade student, fourteen-year-old Annie is coast-
ing through high school with Cs and Ds, despite excellent scores on abil-
ity and achievement tests. Although her grades were satisfactory in
elementary and middle school, they dropped dramatically in ninth grade
and have been marginal ever since. Annie's sister, Sarah, a high school
senior, is an honor roll student and has been accepted at a top state uni-
versity. After Annie graduates from high school, she wants to move to
Los Angeles and "get into the music business." Currently, she is
putting forth just enough effort to pass the subjects she dislikes or con-
siders irrelevant, which is most of them. When her parents try to talk to
her about the value of getting an education, Annie either tunes them
out or storms angrily out of the room. Her parents are so distressed that
they frequently argue about how to deal with their daughter. Both se-
cretly wonder if their marriage will survive her high school years.

All three of these youngsters are underachievers. Underachievers can
be found in every grade in school, from kindergarten to graduate
school, in both sexes, across ethnic and socioeconomic groups, and in
every occupation. What is underachievement? Underachievement is a
discrepancy between ability and performance *that persists over time.* Underachievers do not wake up one morning and suddenly decide not to
do their work. Nor do they wake up after years of performing poorly in
school and suddenly decide to change—not without understanding and
help. Underachievement can occur at any level of intellectual ability.
Some underachievers are gifted, with superior intellectual ability and
special talents. Others have mild to severe learning problems that are
compounded by their lack of effort in the classroom. In a sense, we are
all underachievers. Every individual, by virtue of being human and being born to less-than-perfect parents in a less-than-perfect world, is
something of an underachiever.

Underachievement can reveal itself as early as preschool, or it may
first surface at transitional points, such as second grade, fourth grade,
seventh grade, the first year of high school, or even later. All too often,

however, the early warning signs of underachievement are overlooked or minimized by parents and teachers. The progression of under-achievement is often so insidious that many children, especially those who are very bright, highly verbal, or both, are not identified until late in their school careers. Nevertheless, careful observation reveals the operation of the child's maladaptive views of the self and others, even in the early elementary grades.

THE UNDERACHIEVER IN ELEMENTARY SCHOOL: EARLY WARNING SIGNS

Mrs. Finch is conducting a reading group in a corner of the room with six first graders while the other pupils work on the morning's indepen-dent assignments. Greg, a pudgy, freckle-faced youngster, twirls his pencil and wiggles restlessly in his chair. As he looks at his papers, an anxious expression comes over his face. He begins drumming on his desk with his pencil, first softly, then louder and louder until Mrs. Finch looks in his direction.

"Greg, stop making that noise!" she commands.

Looking abashed, Greg stops drumming, but he still does not begin working. After a few seconds, he picks up one of his papers, leaps out of his chair, startling the children seated near him by the sudden move-ment, and walks back to Mrs. Finch.

"Greg, why are you here?" asks Mrs. Finch in an impatient tone.

"I don't know how to do this," he mumbles, waving the paper in her direction.

"Where were you when I was giving directions?" demands the teacher. "You know there are to be no interruptions while I'm having a reading group!"

Rebuffed, Greg trudges slowly back to his seat. Even now, however, he does not begin to work. After a moment, he reaches into his desk, pulls out two small action figures, and begins to enact a battle with them. The fighting becomes fast and furious, but because it is con-ducted in silence, the teacher does not notice. Greg's papers lie un-touched on his desk.

Here, even in first grade, the operation of the budding under-achiever's distorted internal perspective—and its devastating effects on his classroom performance—are already apparent. Because he believes that he is incompetent, he feels incapable of performing tasks on his own. But because he also believes that others will be unavailable or un-helpful if he seeks assistance, he unconsciously behaves in such a way that he induces those very reactions. Unaware of the maladaptive be-liefs underlying his irritating behavior, his teacher responds in the re-jecting manner he anticipates, further confirming his negative views of himself and others.

As the deleterious effects of the child's internal world become more and more apparent in the classroom, parents may attempt to reassure each other and themselves by downplaying or normalizing his inappro-priate behavior, especially when the underachiever is a boy.

Renardo, who had been a happy-go-lucky youngster in the warm, play-ful atmosphere of his kindergarten class, was overwhelmed by the aca-demic requirements of first grade, a demanding teacher, and the loss of his status as the smartest youngster in his class. By October, he was acting out his anger and frustration by distracting himself and others when the teacher gave instructions, failing to complete his work, and even provoking fights with other students.

"I know Renardo isn't paying attention and is acting up a little in class, but are those really such serious problems at his age?" inquired Mrs. Johnson, a hopeful tone in her voice. "I've been talking with my friends who have children, and they say you just have to expect boys to get into trouble in school."

Inattention, lack of productivity, and aggressive behavior are most definitely *not* normal. They represent the child's unconscious attempt to communicate to his parents and teachers that he is feeling over-whelmed by his school experiences—and that he desperately needs their help. Although the underachiever is often able to maintain ade-quate grades during elementary school because of his intellectual gifts, the signs of the latent underachievement syndrome become increas-ingly observable over time:

- Performs well when given one-to-one attention but is restless and unproductive when required to work independently
- Has trouble beginning and completing tasks
- Withdraws attention when parents or teachers give instructions
- Becomes distractible and distracting when not the center of attention
- Has difficulty relating positively to peers (may be revealed in complaints that others are "bothering" the child)
- Has difficulty relating positively to siblings
- Displays frequent temper outbursts or abrupt mood changes
- Makes incessant demands but is never satisfied with anything for very long
- Requires caretaking on some tasks beyond the age when it is appropriate
- Has difficulty organizing school materials and belongings at home

The Downward Drift Begins

Because the fundamentals of reading, mathematics, and written language are taught in the early grades, underachievement that goes untreated or is treated unsuccessfully in elementary school has devastating effects on the child's academic progress. Gaps in important skills, concepts, and problem-solving strategies incurred through inattention and lack of practice make subsequent learning much more difficult and may never be fully remedied. Lack of appropriate intervention leads to further declines in achievement, setting in motion the child's downward drift in the educational system, a process that, tragically, can begin as early as first grade.

Mrs. Parker dabbed at her eyes with a tissue as she reread the note from her daughter's teacher. "Miss Smith says that she wants to move Curtissa down another reading group. I don't understand what's happened! Curtissa did so well in kindergarten last year! Miss Smith says she doesn't pay attention in class or finish her assignments. I know she can do the work that the top reading group is doing, I just know she can!" She fumbled in her purse for another tissue.

Untreated, underachievement in the elementary years not only interferes with mastery of later academic tasks, it has a profoundly negative effect on the child's view of himself as a learner. The underachiever does not just fail to acquire basic skills and knowledge. He learns that he is unsuccessful in the most important task of his young life: being a student. Even very young children quickly begin to think of themselves as dumb, slow, and bad if they are unable to make satisfactory progress in school. These painful feelings are then acted out in battles between parent and child at home and teacher and child at school over the smallest requests for independent effort—effort that the child fears may be unsuccessful.

"It takes forever to get Henry ready for school in the morning," complained his mother. "His books and materials are scattered all around his bedroom, and there he is in front of the TV watching cartoons while I'm trying to fix his lunch. And he still needs me to tie his shoes. When I tell him he's eight years old and big enough to do it himself, he just keeps whining for me to help him until I give in."

THE UNDERACHIEVER IN MIDDLE SCHOOL

During the middle school years, the manifestations of the underachievement pattern change somewhat under the developmental pressures of approaching adolescence. Overactivity and restlessness decline, often to be replaced by a dreamy detachment that is just as detrimental to learning and performance. Overt opposition in the classroom may also subside, leaving a passive, covert hostility that is equally successful in resisting teachers' pressure for productivity. At home, the underachiever becomes moodier, more irritable, and increasingly resentful of her parents' efforts to motivate her.

"I just don't know what to do about Larry," confessed his father, shaking his head regretfully. "He's not applying himself in school, but any time his mother or I try to talk to him about it, he complains that we're 'bugging him' and shuts us off. If we keep trying, we end up in a shouting match. I guess it's just a stage he's going through, but he's making family life miserable for everyone right now."

These behaviors—and the underachievement syndrome from which they arise—are *not* indicative of a time-limited stage through which the child is passing and from which she will eventually recover. On the contrary, the middle school underachiever who does not receive appropriate assistance develops into a high school underachiever whose maladaptive habits and attitudes are even more firmly entrenched. The warning signs of underachievement in middle school include:

- Interprets suggestions, advice, and feedback as criticism
- Displays excessive sensitivity about her own feelings but lacks empathy for the feelings of others
- Adopts an "I don't care" attitude about achievement
- Shows a shift in patterns of friendship toward lower-achieving peers
- Begins to restrict communication with family members about her thoughts and feelings, especially those related to her school experiences
- Often complains that teachers are unfair, mean, and "dumb"
- Shows an increasing specialization of effort, with satisfactory, even excellent, performance in one or two subjects or extracurricular areas and mediocre performance in the rest
- Lacks the capacity to entertain herself and complains constantly of being bored at school and at home
- Complains that others in the family receive more attention or material objects than she does
- Assigns blame to others for her own problems

As the child moves through the middle school years, changes in the curriculum and greater demands for autonomy conspire to reveal the latent underachievement pattern. With competence in reading taken for granted, formal reading instruction typically disappears by seventh grade, to be replaced by instruction in grammar and literature. At the same time, demands for independent reading in the various subject areas dramatically increase. The underachiever who spent her time daydreaming or being disruptive during first and second grades, when the basics of phonics and reading comprehension are taught, finds that she has trouble decoding the words in her textbooks, much less understanding and applying what she has read. Similarly, the departmentalized nature of instruction in middle school means that the underachiever must now cope with several teachers and several classroom changes instead of one or two. Although departmentalization exposes the child to a larger number of potentially helpful attachment figures, it also reduces her opportunity to use her teachers as secure bases because she spends less time with each of them. Moreover, the youngster who had difficulty keeping up with her classroom materials when she spent most of her day at one desk in one room must suddenly manage a locker and six or seven sets of books, notebooks, handouts, and assignments. Once in the classroom, she spends most of her day listening to whole-class instruction or working independently, when paying attention and persisting on her own are the very two skills in which she is most deficient.

Meanwhile, the underachiever's continuing mediocre academic performance and petulance, opposition, or demandingness at home and in the classroom make it more and more obvious that something is wrong. At school, teachers try to coax, lecture, or nag her into better performance and behavior. At home, the battle over homework intensifies. But the more parents and teachers urge the child to try harder, the more the voices of her internal world cry out that she is bad and incompetent and does not deserve to succeed or receive help from others. Because her anxious parents and teachers do not understand her internal perspective, they feel rejected and angry at her lack of response to their efforts to help her be more successful. Gradually they become more negative and controlling, and the child becomes more resistant in return, trapped in a vicious cycle of failure, rejection, and alienation. Now the child feels bad for two reasons: first, because she cannot be the kind of successful student she longs to be, and second, because she has disappointed the parents and teachers she wishes so much to please. Small wonder that she has little energy left for her schoolwork.

In his sixth-grade classroom, Derrick usually complied with the teacher's instructions, but he put forth only as much effort as was absolutely necessary to scrape by. Nor did he complete most of the assignments he took home.

"Mom asks me all the time about how I'm doing in school," he related in a dejected tone. "When I don't do my work, she gets upset and reminds me of how much she wants me to get a good education. It makes me feel really bad about the way my grades are." As he slumped lower in his chair, his tired expression and depressed posture made him look older than his eleven years.

Although middle school presents the underachiever with an expanding array of choices in terms of coursework and extracurricular activities, her parents notice that she seems to be deliberately circumscribing her educational experiences. Instead of using middle school as a platform for launching herself in new and exciting directions, the underachiever seeks to avoid her perceived inadequacies in favor of concentrating on the fewer and fewer areas in which she is proficient. She talks about wanting to be on the softball team but never gets around to signing up. Or her grades may be so poor that she may be ineligible to participate in any sport. She agrees that the Drama Club might be interesting, but when her parents ask why she hasn't joined, she tells them, "That's dumb stuff." Rather than take an additional elective class, she opts for a study hall. Close observation reveals that she is carefully noncompetitive, avoiding leadership positions even in areas she enjoys. Confronted by her parents and teachers with her lack of effort, she denies concern about her poor grades and states that she "just wants to be average" or doesn't care about "that dumb old math."

Beginning in middle school, the underachiever often tries to shore up her self-esteem by focusing excessively on her peers rather than participating in academics, sports, or other activities in which competition—and evaluation—are inevitable. Alarmed parents realize that they are well acquainted with fewer and fewer of the underachiever's friends, much less their parents, and that many of those friends also seem to be underachieving in school and having trouble developing meaningful educational and career plans. In her desperate search for some form of validation, the underachiever may attach to a peer group that, because of the insecurities of its members, fails to support achievement. On the contrary, members are implicitly discouraged from working to raise their grades because such improvement would excite envy and anxiety about their own lack of accomplishment. Often they have special labels with which to designate and ostracize achievers: nerds, geeks, dweebs, eggheads, and so on. Membership in an antiachievement peer group also helps underachievers deny that they have a problem. Basking in the glow of peer acceptance, they find it easier to shrug off their teachers' and parents' concern about the seriousness of their academic situation.

> *"Look, I'm just not into school, OK? I'm making Cs and that's fine with me. Cs aren't bad," protested twelve-year-old Joan, tossing her long dark hair back with a disarming smile. "I just wish Dad agreed with me."*

But as the child's work habits and performance become more and more dysfunctional, the feedback she and her parents receive from the school becomes increasingly negative. Teachers tell the parents, "She's smart but she's lazy. She's got to buckle down and study harder. You need to make her take more responsibility for her work." Unfortunately, this kind of advice gives neither parents nor child any meaningful help. On the contrary, it further diminishes the child's flagging self-esteem and the parents' sense of competence as parents. When children are unable to develop good feelings about themselves as students and to feel positively about others who are guiding their learning experiences, they are likely to abandon the effort to obtain satisfaction from school. Instead, to defend against the depression and anger they are feeling at their lack of success, they may seek immediate gratification from external sources, such as attention from peers, alcohol or drugs, or risk taking, rather than rely on healthy, self-generated gratifications that foster personal growth. The child who has not developed an internal image of herself as an active agent involved in an ever-increasing mastery of her environment develops an inner emptiness that makes her vulnerable to exploitation by others and to the desire to exploit others to gain some sense of mastery.

THE ASSIGNMENT OF BLAME

Underachievement that is not identified and treated impairs not only the child's educational development but also the relationship between parent and child, the marital relationship, and the atmosphere in the family as a whole. After years of unsuccessfully trying to help their child, parents feel anxious and discouraged about their own ability and worth as parents. They may think, Why is my child doing poorly in school when other children are doing well? What am I doing wrong? What is my spouse doing wrong? What's wrong with my child? All too often, that anxiety and frustration turn to anger. They begin blaming themselves, each other, the child's teachers, and the child himself for not being able to solve the problem.

This assignment of blame only makes matters worse. In a two-parent family, accusations deprive both parents of the psychological support so desperately needed in the helping process. A single parent already lacking support for parenting may blame him- or herself, compounding the self-doubt and anguish that so often accompany divorce. At the same time, the frustration parents direct against the school makes it all the more difficult for them to team with the child's teachers. Instead of working to understand and solve the problem together, parents and teachers may end up so alienated from each other that cooperation is impossible. Similarly, the underachiever who is told that he is the source of the problem and needs to straighten up and get his act together is helped only to find a focus outside himself at which to direct his negative feelings: his unempathic parents. The emotional distance between parents and child looms larger with each passing year.

THE UNDERACHIEVER IN HIGH SCHOOL

Regardless of how unsuccessful the underachiever has been in elementary and middle school, he and his parents are seldom prepared for the shock of the transition from the relatively sheltered and nurturing environment of middle school to the impersonal world of high school. First, the underachiever entering high school is almost certain to suffer from academic skill deficits that have gone unnoticed and unremedied, so that he finds himself in classes that may be an appropriate match for his ability but are considerably over his head in terms of his achievement. Moreover, his poor study habits and behaviors, which his middle school teachers may have accommodated to some degree, are suddenly no longer tolerated. He is expected to assume responsibility for his academic work or suffer the consequences.

> "I can't believe it! I didn't turn in my English project on the exact day it was due, and then Mrs. Barnett wouldn't accept it at all!" complained a shocked and angry ninth grader. "Back in middle school, teachers used to let us hand in late work. Now I'm going to flunk English for the six weeks!"

At the same time that the underachiever is struggling to cope with the greater rigor of his school situation, he is confronted with the full force of the developmental challenges presented by adolescence. Not only must he move out into the world and achieve greater independence from his family, he must make a series of educational and career decisions that will have a profound impact on the rest of his life. To the underachiever, who possesses so few internal resources to sustain him through this difficult period, these tasks are not exciting challenges to be mastered but additional opportunities for defeat and humiliation. And who is available in his new learning environment to guide him on his perilous journey? As much as his teachers may want to help, they must concentrate on meeting the daily instructional needs of 120 or 150 different youngsters. His guidance counselors are just as overwhelmed with mountains of paperwork and all too many troubled students who need their immediate attention.

"You want to know how students get to see the guidance counselors in this school?" asked one overworked and overwrought counselor. "Well, it helps to be suicidal!"

Unable to ask for the support he so desperately needs, the underachiever reacts with anger and despair.

Marty leaned far over the high school conference table in his agitation. "It's awful in ninth grade," he said bitterly. "They just dump you up here and forget about you. They expect you to be able to get along on your own. Nobody really cares what you do."

The combination of the pressures of adolescence and the demands of the high school environment produces the following signs of underachievement during this period:

- Has trouble using teachers and other school staff as sources of support
- Fails to develop meaningful educational and career goals
- Engages in a pattern of self-defeating behavior with regard to educational or career planning (for example, "forgets" to ask for recommendations from school counselor for college application)
- Increasingly withdraws from the family in favor of relying on peers for approval
- Becomes attached to an antiachievement peer group or a group that focuses excessively on socializing rather than on achieving
- Becomes overly involved with one or two relationships to the exclusion of others
- Displays clowning or defiant behavior in school, especially in classes that are outside the underachiever's perceived competence
- Withdraws from competitive and evaluative situations
- Suffers from chronic feelings of anxiety and depression about his lack of success, masked by an "I don't care" attitude

- May turn to external sources of stimulation, such as drugs and alcohol, to relieve feelings of emptiness

The high school years can wreak havoc on the underachiever's relationship with his parents as well as on his educational and career prospects. Although some contention between parents and teenagers is part of the process of growing up, the underachiever's tendency to perceive others as unreliable and unhelpful can turn every attempt at communication into a confrontation. To parents, it can seem as if their child has vanished, leaving an inaccessible and incomprehensible alien in his place, while to the underachiever, it seems as if his parents are less capable of understanding him than ever. Parent and child alike feel overwhelmed, angry, and desperate, and each in his own way comes to believe that there is no support to be had from other family members.

"When I get home from school, I throw my books on the bed, hit the refrigerator, and get ready to meet my friends just as soon as I can," recounted Ryan. "When Mom asks me where I'm going, I just say, 'Out,' and take off before she can get on my case about anything."

Ryan's mother had a different version of her son's behavior. "He acts like this is a hotel instead of a home," she said despairingly. "He comes in after school for something to eat and goes out and we don't see him again until eleven o'clock or later that night. If his father or I try to talk to him about it, he just doesn't pay any attention."

As parents often discover to their distress, the high school years not only herald an expanded range of educational options, they offer additional opportunities for the underachiever to act out his distorted internal belief system. Today's teenagers seem to have an unlimited number of ways of expressing unhappiness and lack of direction. The underachiever who has been inattentive and hyperactive at school and irritable and defiant at home is likely to expand his negative behavioral repertoire as he gets older. The seven-year-old who comforts himself for a perceived rejection by his teacher by playing secretly with action figures instead of doing his classwork may evolve into a sixteen-year-old who cuts classes, abuses drugs or alcohol, or engages in delinquent behavior to defend against his feelings of inadequacy.

As the high school years proceed, the underachiever's self-defeating behaviors are likely to become more entrenched because of his increasing dependence on the peer group for comfort and validation. Although all adolescents are susceptible to peer pressure, the underachiever, with his meager supply of self-esteem, is especially vulnerable. To gain some sense of validation, the underachiever may take on the role of school rebel or class clown, giving up on the effort to obtain adult approval in favor of approval from peers. Unfortunately, in an antiachievement peer group, approval is assured for certain kinds of antiauthoritarian behaviors, many of which interfere with achievement not only for the underachiever but also for his classmates. But the temporary increase in self-esteem the adolescent obtains for his defiant performance soon recedes, leaving him feeling empty and despairing again, because validation earned for negative behavior cannot construct an internal image of the self as a lovable, capable person.

Mike lunges into class as the final seconds of the bell are echoing, clutching his books in one hand. He pulls up short at the teacher's desk, does an elaborate double take, and then, grinning broadly, proceeds to his seat with a peculiar loping stride, setting down his feet very quietly but taking very long steps. The walk is both comical and defiant. The teacher, Mr. Dobbins, ignores him, but the class titters.

"Class, clear your desks and get ready for your science test," orders Mr. Dobbins.

A look of anxiety crosses briefly over Mike's face, quickly to be replaced with his former grin. He leans over to a classmate and asks in a stage whisper, "Whaaat test?"

"We have a test on Chapter Four today," his classmate whispers back.

"OH NOOOOO!" wails Mike, clutching his head in his hands in a highly dramatic gesture, and the students giggle again.

"That will be enough," chides Mr. Dobbins as he passes out the test papers. After a minute or two, Mike gets out of his seat and begins to

sharpen five pencils, one after another, at the pencil sharpener in the front of the room. When the teacher tells him to sharpen just one pencil and sit down, he protests, "But, Mr. D., I need all these pencils." His smile changes to a frown and he stomps noisily back to his seat and slams down his pencils on his desk. The long-suffering Mr. Dobbins writes up a disciplinary referral and sends him to the in-school suspension room to finish his test. Once there, Mike refuses to work.

Girls can be just as susceptible as boys to the antiachievement attitudes of peers.

"I don't want to do too well, you know," explained fifteen-year-old Sherry, an extremely attractive and talented student with a C average. "My friends might think I was a nerd and really out of it. And guys don't like girls who think about nothing but school. I know my parents care about my grades, but right now my friends are what's most important to me."

Thus in a vicious cycle, the underachiever's failure to earn validation for his academic performance leads to his increasing reliance on peer validation to bolster his pitifully small supply of self-esteem. Planning for his educational or career future is neglected in favor of frenzied efforts to maintain the attachment with peers.

"I just can't get Grace motivated to begin looking at colleges," moaned her distraught mother. "Here she is at the end of her tenth-grade year, and she has no more idea of where she wants to go or what she wants to do than her nine-year-old brother. All she wants to do is go to the mall with her friends! I've sent for nearly a dozen college catalogs, and I don't think she's looked at any of them!"

RESTRICTION OF EDUCATIONAL AND CAREER CHOICES

The effects of untreated underachievement on the high school underachiever's educational and career options are inevitable—and devastating. The parents' dream (and often, the underachiever's secret dream, too, however much he may deny it) of an Ivy League school or a first-rate state university fades as the months and years of poor academic performance continue. The underachiever's first line of defense is to protest that he doesn't care about attending "that place for geeks and tech-heads." After a while, he may claim that he doesn't want to go to college at all. Post–high school plans are vague or take the form of escapist, grandiose fantasies such as moving far from home (New York City and Los Angeles are favorite choices, depending on their proximity to the underachiever) and becoming a performing artist, such as a rock star or actor. Playing pro sports is another favorite pipe dream, although it gradually fades away in the face of the underachiever's inability to apply himself conscientiously to master a sport or cooperate with teammates and coaches any more than he can apply himself to his studies or cooperate with his teachers and parents.

As the months and years go by, his parents' hopes that "at last he'll see that it's time to buckle down" become dimmer and dimmer. Most high school underachievers do manage to live up to at least one expectation, however: their own belief that they are incompetent and no one can help them. Sadly, by the time they graduate (if they do) from high school, they may no longer be underachievers. They have lost so many opportunities for learning and practice that their potential has irrevocably been diminished. They have been transformed from underachievers into low achievers.

THE UNDERACHIEVER IN ADULTHOOD

Because underachievement is a chronic, pervasive condition rather than a stage through which children pass and from which they emerge unscathed, without help, the pattern persists into adulthood. All of us have encountered bright, talented individuals who, despite their early promise, just can't seem to "get their act together" and are leading unsatisfying, unproductive lives. These individuals suffer from incessant boredom, feelings of restlessness and emptiness, and the firm conviction that the world has failed to give them their just reward. Although at first glance they may seem to be invested in some social or political cause, it gradually becomes apparent that they drift from cause to cause and show no real commitment to anything or anyone. They may hold marginal, low-paying positions without leadership responsibility in industries or organizations that they once aspired to lead, or they may defend against the disappointment of their former ambitions by seeking employment outside the realm of their own interests. Some continue to try to satisfy their unmet needs for security and validation by working on grandiose creative projects out of the public eye—composing, playing, or writing year after year in obscurity. But the music never finds an audience, and the poems and plays are never submitted for publication. The great American novel never gets written, and the great American actor never gets discovered. In the end, these underachievers and the nation they could have served so well as creative, productive citizens have both lost something of incalculable value.

2.

Identifying the Underachiever

At this point, parents may be wondering, "Can my child do better in school? He certainly shows some of the warning signs of underachievement. Should I be concerned? And how can I tell if he's an underachiever or if he has some other problem?"

It is my experience in many years of working with underachievers that when parents believe their child's academic performance does not reflect his true ability, they are invariably correct. Parents rather than teachers are usually the first to recognize that the child is underachieving, especially in today's schools where the increasing number of children with learning and behavior problems makes it less and less likely that youngsters who are making Cs and Ds when they could be making As and Bs or who are making poor grades but are not exhibiting flagrantly disruptive behavior will be singled out for special attention and help.

Sometimes when parents are convinced that their child can do better academically, they are met with understanding by school personnel, who work with the parents to try to solve the problem. Unfortunately, however, parents' efforts to obtain assistance are frequently greeted with well-meaning but inappropriate advice. If the child is in elementary school, they are likely to be told, "He's just immature. He'll grow out of it." The younger the child, the more likely are parents to be given such "developmental immaturity" explanations. When the same problems arise again the following year, the same "immaturity" explanations are offered. Only after the child has displayed several years of mediocre grades may the school finally acknowledge that something must be wrong and initiate an evaluation. Many of the parents of middle and high school underachievers with whom I have worked and whose children did *not* grow out of their problems were told something like this for years, wasting precious time when treatment could have been initiated. Uncertain of what to think or do, the parents may continue trying to reassure each other and themselves that their child will "grow out of it" until finally one day in ninth or tenth grade, the child's underachievement, now a chronic, firmly entrenched syndrome, can no longer be denied. The years that have elapsed between the parents' initial nagging doubts and the beginning of treatment take a terrible toll on the underachieving child's academic skills, self-esteem, educational and occupational prospects, and the parent-child relationship itself.

Rather than waiting for the school to take action, parents should initiate the assessment process *as soon as they suspect their child may be an underachiever.* As we shall see, however, identifying underachievement is not as simple as it sounds.

> *"Tommy has mastered 50 percent of the second grade reading and math objectives. He takes part in class discussions, but he has trouble paying attention and completing written work."* Mr. Matthews tossed his eight-year-old son's report card on the table and shook his head with exasperation. *"What does all that mean? Is he having some kind of problem or not?"*

How can parents tell if their child is an underachiever? By definition, underachievement is a discrepancy between intellectual ability and academic achievement, so that a child who has average or above-average ability but below-average achievement is an underachiever. Intellectual ability is usually measured by IQ or aptitude test scores, along with teacher and parent observations, while achievement is measured by classroom grades or scores on standardized achievement tests. Determining whether a child is underachieving sounds perfectly straightforward.

In actual practice, however, it can be very difficult for parents to determine whether their child is, in fact, doing the best that he can academically. The problem of identifying underachievement is especially acute in the elementary school for several reasons. In the first place, some districts do not administer group ability and achievement tests at that level or administer them only once over the elementary school years, making it impossible to detect the presence of higher ability than the child's grades would suggest or a persistent pattern of underachievement. Second, because students in many elementary schools are evaluated by means of checks indicating mastery of grade-level objectives rather than letter grades based on group comparisons, parents may receive little or no information to help them assess the adequacy of their child's performance relative to other children his age or in terms of his own intellectual potential. Moreover, elementary school teachers may try so hard to be positive in their written comments on report cards that they unintentionally lull parents into a false sense of security about the child's progress. Fortunately, most underachievers can be identified as early as kindergarten and certainly by second grade, where changes in the curriculum and organization of instruction reveal the previously unrecognized pattern. All too often, however, even concerned and attentive parents fail to recognize that their child is underachieving.

DELAYS IN IDENTIFYING UNDERACHIEVERS

The Search for a Nonpsychological Cause of Underachievement

In addition to school factors that may delay the identification of underachievement, there are several reasons why parents themselves may have trouble identifying their child as an underachiever. First, parents who secretly fear that someone will blame them and their parenting for the child's poor school performance may waste valuable time searching for a physical rather than a psychological basis for her underachievement. Unfortunately, there is such a wealth of misguided advice for parents of children with learning and behavior problems that parents seeking a physical reason for the child's underachievement can generally find one that is plausible enough to satisfy them if they persist long enough. The "causes" of underachievement I have encountered over the years include allergies, food additives, hypersensitivity to sound, early onset of puberty, late onset of puberty, hormonal imbalance, low metabolism, high metabolism, visual tracking problems, and a host of others, all with a physical cause and a medical solution. Although biological factors *can* affect academic performance, parents may become trapped in a futile search for a nonpsychological cause of underachievement to avoid considering that ineffective family interactional patterns may be contributing to the child's difficulties.

Despite these cautionary notes, the first step of the assessment process should be a complete physical examination for the child by a competent pediatrician. Parents should take the time to explain to the child why she is having a physical examination and describe any procedures involved. Children whose parents are searching for a physical rather than psychological explanation of their underachievement are especially likely to harbor confused notions about why they are going to the doctor.

Jeffrey, an underachieving ten-year-old fifth grader, appeared subdued as he entered the guidance office. "I've got to leave school early today," he told me. "Mom's taking me to the doctor. I think it's about my blood or something." He looked down anxiously at his hands, as if they might provide some clue as to what might be wrong with him.

If the child appears to have difficulty seeing or hearing, parents should also have the child evaluated by an ophthalmologist or audiologist. Such evaluations occasionally reveal problems in visual or auditory acuity or perception. In the vast majority of cases, however, the search for physical causes does not uncover anything medically significant and only delays the treatment process.

DIFFERENCES IN HOME AND SCHOOL BEHAVIOR

"Antony's teacher says he's not paying attention in class and doesn't get his work done on time," Mrs. Sabatini reported, a worried expression

on her face. "She says if this keeps up, she'll have to recommend that he repeat second grade. But we don't see those kinds of problems at home. Do you think his teacher just doesn't know how to motivate students?"

Another cause of delays in identifying and treating underachievers is that children's behavior at home and at school can be very different. It is not uncommon for children who are distractible or disruptive at school to behave appropriately (or at least manageably) at home most of the time. When the teacher approaches the parents about the child's inattentiveness, lack of effort, or misbehavior, they may dismiss her concern because their perception of the child is so different.

These differences in perception may be partly a result of the parents' desire to avoid seeing the child's ineffective behaviors. Struggling to cope with their own responsibilities and worries, they have a hard time hearing that something else in their lives is not going right. Differences between parents' and teachers' views of the child may also stem from the different demands of the home and school environments for attention, responsibility, and productivity. Many of today's overburdened parents have precious little time and energy to monitor their child's behavior closely. Moreover, they may find it easier to manage chores themselves and require the child to make few if any contributions to the household. The child who spends most of her time at home sitting in front of the television or playing video games is likely to be a child who spends most of her time at school waiting for her teacher to motivate her or searching for external stimulation. Thus parents may fail to see the negative behaviors that are keeping the child from success in school, or they may fail to understand the relevance of these behaviors to achievement.

UNDERACHIEVEMENT—
OR SOME OTHER PROBLEM?

Identifying underachievement is also complicated because many conditions can contribute to a child's poor school performance. Asking themselves the following questions should help parents determine whether their child is an underachiever or is experiencing some other type of learning or emotional problem.

1. *Is the child's underachievement her major problem, or is she having trouble in other important areas of functioning as well?*

Parents should ask themselves whether the child has difficulty forming interpersonal relationships and mastering basic developmental tasks in addition to her difficulty achieving in school. Such children are likely to be suffering from general developmental delays rather than just academic underachievement. Referral to a psychologist specializing in developmental disorders for a comprehensive assessment of the child's intellectual, social, and emotional functioning is in order.

2. *Is the child's underachievement general or specific?*

Is the child doing poorly in all or most of her subjects or only in one or two areas? Underachievers' performance tends to vary, often dramatically, from subject to subject. Underachievers usually do much better in highly structured subjects such as mathematics than in subjects such as social studies and science that require them to generate their own structure and organization for many assignments. They also perform poorly on tasks that require planning and persistence, such as long-term projects and creative-writing assignments.

In addition, parents should consider whether variations in the child's underachievement are related to differences in teachers rather than differences in subjects. Careful examination may reveal that she achieves at a satisfactory or superior level when she likes her teacher but performs poorly when she does not. Achievement that fluctuates with the teacher rather than with the academic subject suggests a motivational rather than a learning problem.

3. *Has the onset of the child's poor academic performance been sudden or gradual?*

The difference between a sudden drop in school performance and a pattern of chronic, insidious underachievement is critical to accurate identification. If parents are able to identify a recent stressor, such as parental separation or divorce, illness or death of a family member, or birth of a sibling in conjunction with a decline in grades, the child's poor performance may be a response to that event. Such stressors can trigger temporary underachievement in any child.

Parents should also look for a combination of stressors that may seem insignificant to adults but that can be overwhelming concerns in the mind of a child. These include a move from a familiar home, school, or neighborhood; the death of a beloved pet; and the loss of an important peer relationship, such as a close friend moving away. Depression in children is often masked by other behaviors. The child may not show her grief openly, especially if her parents have trouble coping with painful feelings themselves. Instead, her sadness may be expressed in irritability, agitation, or difficulty beginning and completing tasks, with lower grades the result.

Mr. and Mrs. McCowan were very distressed at their daughter's sudden drop in grades at the beginning of her fifth-grade year. Patty had entered the school in the fall of that year following the family's move from another part of the state. Although Patty was well liked by her teachers and classmates and seemed to be making a good adjustment socially, her grades were significantly lower compared with her previous achievement. Her parents also noted that she was having more physical complaints, especially headaches.

As the McCowans talked about their concerns in a conference with me and her teachers, they realized that Patty was reacting to the family's relocation. The move had occurred at the beginning of fifth grade, a time when peer friendships become vitally important to children. The McCowans recalled that Patty had just acquired a best friend during the summer before the move. With their new awareness of Patty's loss, her parents suggested that she telephone her friend and plan a visit the following summer. Recognizing that her parents understood her distress and were supporting her efforts to maintain contact with her old friends, Patty gave up her underachievement, which represented not only grief but also a way of maintaining attachments to her former school and classmates. Her depression lifted, she began reaching out to her peers and teachers, and her grades returned to their previous level.

UNDERACHIEVER OR GIFTED AND BORED?

"Jamie's just plain bored with school," explained Mr. Simpson, the father of a severely underachieving sixth grader. "If they'd put him in the gifted program where he'd be challenged, he'd do much better."

Parents of underachievers sometimes wonder if their children are gifted youngsters who are just plain bored with school. As much as we would like to think otherwise, school often *is* boring, especially for very bright children. How can parents tell whether their child's poor grades are due to the boredom of a bright, unchallenged student or to underachievement?

It is certainly true that if children are not intellectually challenged at school, they may lose motivation and achieve at a mediocre level. Placement in a gifted program may inspire a few underachievers to work harder, by offering a heightened sense of self-worth, a highly stimulating curriculum, and an achievement-oriented peer group. For the vast majority of underachievers, however, placement in a gifted program without additional interventions won't turn them into achievers. Because a child's motivation is primarily related to his internal beliefs, not to external school factors, a change of placement cannot provide the motivational fuel necessary for high achievement. Moreover, it is naive to expect that a simple program change will be capable of wiping out years of maladaptive study habits, attitudes, and behaviors without changes in the way in which significant individuals in the child's life interact with him.

On the contrary, placement in a gifted program can make underachievement worse by increasing academic and psychological demands on the child to the point that his anxiety becomes unmanageable. The result can be an outbreak of misbehavior in a previously well-behaved child, a precipitous drop in achievement, or both.

"I don't know what to do with Teddy anymore," said the fifth-grade gifted-class teacher anxiously. "He's just bouncing off the walls these days. I know he doesn't mean to misbehave, but he gets so wound up, and he sets all the other students off, too. And now he's forgetting to do his homework. I'd like to recommend him for the middle school gifted program next year, but I just don't know if he—or the teacher—can take it!"

A youngster with superior ability, Teddy had been placed in gifted programs throughout his school years. Now, however, the combination of the greater demands of the fifth-grade curriculum and the impending transition to middle school had increased his anxiety to the point that he was no longer able to cope.

UNDERACHIEVER OR LEARNING DISABLED?

Today the problem of underachievement is often "solved" by assigning the child a label: learning disabilities (LD), Attention-Deficit/Hyperactivity Disorder (ADHD), or both. In the case of LD, the "solution" is placement in special education. In the case of ADHD, the "solution" to the child's problem is a drug.

Before the 1960s, the term *learning disabilities* (LD) was unknown. In 1975, Public Law 94–142, the Education for All Handicapped Children Act, recognized LD as a handicapping condition, allocated federal funds for school programs, and declared that free educational services must be provided to all LD children. Since that time, millions of children have been diagnosed as having learning disabilities and placed in special education programs mandated to serve them. Depending on the definition, estimates of children with LD range from 3 percent to 15 percent, with many more boys identified than girls.

More than twenty years later, a satisfactory and agreed-upon definition remains elusive. The federal definition of LD included in PL 94–142 states:

"Specific learning disability" means a disorder in one or more of the basic psychological processes involved in understanding or in using language, spoken or written, which may manifest itself in an imperfect ability to listen, think, read, write, spell, or to do mathematical calcula-

tions. The term includes such conditions as perceptual handicaps, brain injury, minimal brain dysfunction, dyslexia, and developmental aphasia. The term does not include children who have learning problems which are primarily the result of visual, hearing or motor handicaps, of mental retardation, of emotional disturbance, or of environmental, cultural, or economic disadvantage. (United States Office of Education, December 29, 1977, Federal Register, 42, p. 65083)

The law also states that children should be classified as learning disabled only if they have a "severe" discrepancy between intellectual ability and achievement in one or more of seven areas related to mathematical and communication skills, such as written expression, reading comprehension, listening comprehension, mathematics, and oral expression.

Just as there is controversy regarding the definition of LD, so there is controversy about the causes of learning disabilities. Originally, the child's learning difficulties were attributed to the effects of "minimal brain dysfunction" (MBD), meaning that the child had brain abnormalities too minor to be detected by standard medical techniques but serious enough to affect his ability to learn. This concept has largely been abandoned, as research has failed to find meaningful differences between the brain functioning of LD and normal children. Today, many experts in the field conceptualize learning disabilities as a group of disorders characterized by difficulty in processing sensory information and using that information to master important academic, social, and physical developmental tasks, including schoolwork. A child with visual perception problems may have trouble distinguishing between different letters (for example, confusing *b* with *d*), copying material from the chalkboard, or keeping his place in reading. The child with auditory perception difficulties may have trouble distinguishing differences in sounds or understanding and remembering a sequence of directions. Another kind of learning disabilities, which is often found in combination with other forms of LD, consists of fine or gross motor coordination problems. A child with fine motor disabilities may display such problems as an awkward pencil grip and messy handwriting, whereas a child with gross motor disabilities may be clumsy, have an awkward gait, or have trouble riding a bicycle, throwing a ball, or mastering other physical skills.

Because the characteristics of underachievers and LD children overlap considerably, it can be very difficult to distinguish a learning disability from underachievement. Both groups are described as having problems organizing their work, following directions, performing consistently from day to day, completing tasks, and putting their thoughts on paper. If the child seems bright but has trouble completing written assignments, is his problem the result of information-processing problems or maladaptive beliefs about his own ability and the ability of others to help him? To be classified as learning disabled, the child must show a discrepancy between ability and achievement. By definition, therefore, all learning disabled children are underachievers, but not all underachievers are learning disabled. Adding to the confusion is the lack of a uniform standard for diagnosing learning disabilities. Just as there is no agreed-upon definition for LD, so the criteria for placement in an LD program vary from one school division to another and from state to state.

For the vast majority of underachievers, a learning disability is *not* the source of their problem. They are disabled in learning, certainly, but they do not have an information-processing problem that interferes with their ability to do academic work. Unfortunately, however, many underachievers are being incorrectly diagnosed as learning disabled and placed in LD special education programs. Because there is no funding mandated for children who are labeled underachievers, parents and teachers may try to have a child classified LD in order to obtain the additional services that they hope will help him be more successful.

Mrs. Adams came right to the point. "How can I get Willie in that learning disabilities class at the middle school next year? I've heard that class helps kids to get organized, and that's just what he needs." Efforts to encourage her to consider other treatment approaches went unheeded. She proclaimed that she was sick and tired of trying to get him to do his work and demanded that he receive a psychological evaluation to see if he was eligible for special services.

Although the test results showed no real indication of a learning dis-
ability, Mrs. Adams insisted that Willie be placed in an LD resource
room for his sixth-grade year, because his achievement test scores were
significantly below his ability test scores. Not surprisingly, Willie's mid-
dle school grades showed no improvement.

Underachiever or
Attention-Deficit/Hyperactivity Disordered?

Mrs. Rodriguez sounded anxious over the telephone. "Juan's teacher
says that we should take him to a clinic for a psychological evaluation.
She thinks he may have Attention-Deficit/Hyperactivity Disorder. I
know he doesn't pay attention to what's going on in class. Maybe that's
why he's been doing so badly."

Parents of an underachieving child may wonder whether their child
has Attention-Deficit/Hyperactivity Disorder (ADHD). They know
from his teachers and their own experience that he is inattentive, impulsive, and distractible (the chief features of ADHD, according to the
standard manual used by mental health professionals to diagnose mental disorders). Their confusion is understandable. Although experts es-
timate that between 3 percent and 5 percent of children have ADHD,
in recent years, ADHD has become one of the most commonly made
diagnoses in children, especially among boys of school age.

Among the causes of ADHD that have been suggested are delays in
neurological development, stress, allergies, food additives, sugar, and immaturity. ADHD has been treated by a wide range of interventions, including stimulant medication; restriction of sugar or food additives;
vitamin therapy; psychotherapy for child, parent, or both; and behavior
modification. Increasingly, however, treatment for ADHD includes or
consists exclusively of stimulant medication. Stimulant medication
refers to psychostimulant medication, sometimes amphetamines such as
dextroamphetamine (trade name, Dexedrine) but more often methyl-
phenidate (trade name, Ritalin). The major effect of these drugs, which
act on the central nervous system, is to increase the child's ability to pay
attention, although they often decrease aggressive and impulsive behav-

ior as well. Although stimulant medication was once prescribed primarily to reduce hyperactivity, it is increasingly being given to children who are not hyperactive but have trouble paying attention. These children are now diagnosed as having Attention-Deficit/Hyperactivity Disorder, Predominantly Inattentive Type.

Quick Fix for a Complex Problem

One of the most unfortunate aspects of the heightened public awareness of ADHD is that it encourages parents to seek a quick and easy solution to a child's academic and adjustment problems without fully exploring the causes of his maladaptive behaviors. As with learning disabilities, ADHD and underachievement share many characteristics, so that distinguishing between the two syndromes can be very difficult. Most ADHD children, like underachievers, achieve at a level below what would be expected based on their ability. Moreover, like underachievers, children with ADHD have trouble paying attention, organizing their school materials, completing homework assignments, and performing consistently from day to day.

As noted above, parents who have trouble seeing themselves as part of the problem may search for some physical disorder in the child that relieves them of responsibility for his disturbing symptoms. School personnel searching for rapid solutions to a child's disruptive and unproductive behavior may also steer parents toward medical causes and solutions rather than undertake the more difficult process of helping parents examine family interactions that may be limiting the child's ability to achieve. The most tragic aspect of diagnosing an underachieving child as having ADHD is that locating the problem within the child rather than within the context of parent-child interactions ignores not only the real cause of the child's underachievement but its solution as well.

The Effects of Stimulant Medication on Achievement

Parents who believe that treating the underachiever with stimulant medication will solve all of his problems are doomed to disappointment. Although stimulant medication can improve a child's capacity to focus attention and sometimes reduce impulsive behavior as well, it cannot improve his skills in reading, mathematics, or any other academic subject. Nor can it change his motivation to do his work. Precious time can be lost and maladaptive attitudes and behaviors can become entrenched if other interventions are not also explored.

In addition, administering stimulant medication as the sole intervention for poor school performance conveys a powerful negative message to the child about the relative efficacy of his own actions and the power of an external agent—the drug. If a child on Ritalin is exhibiting disruptive or unproductive behavior, teachers and parents are very likely to ask, "Have you taken your pill today?" or "When did you take your last pill?" Such messages imply that the important adults in the child's life believe that the drug, not his own effort, has more control over his actions. Such messages are especially damaging to the underachiever who already harbors an internal image of himself as helpless and incompetent. If the child's behavior improves with stimulant medication, the child, his parents, and teachers are likely to attribute the improvement to the drug rather than his own efforts.

What does the child learn from this approach to problem solving? He learns that solutions to his problems are achieved by relying on outside agents rather than on his own resources. Moreover, everyone has decided that the problem resides in the child and that the child is now "fixed" or as fixed as possible. Disturbances in the family system that have been contributing to the child's inattentiveness, impulsivity, and distractibility remain unaddressed.

Terry was unable to concentrate on his second-grade work. He wandered around the room, fidgeted in his seat, and pestered his classmates. At other times, he would sit gazing into space, a worried expression on his face. Although his parents came in for several conferences with his teacher, Terry's behavior and academic performance did not improve, and he was retained in second grade.

At the beginning of his second year in second grade, retention seemed to have solved the problem. Terry was sailing through his work and making good grades without much effort. By November, however, he was again so restless and moody that his teacher suspected ADHD. Just as she was about to suggest to his parents that they have him evaluated, his father called her to report that the parents had separated and the mother had moved out of the home. He also informed her that they had been having marital problems for some time, although they had never discussed them openly with Terry.

GETTING INFORMATION FROM THE SCHOOL

Parents who know or suspect that they have an underachiever on their hands should not wait until they hear from the teacher to establish communication with the school. Building a positive relationship with the teacher as soon as possible is important not only for obtaining accurate information about the child's classroom performance but also for increasing the teacher's commitment to the treatment process.

Conducting Constructive
Parent-Teacher Conferences

Promptly at 3:15 P.M., Mrs. Reimer appears in Mrs. Davis's fifth-grade classroom to discuss her son, Charlie. Mrs. Davis begins a recitation of her concerns about Charlie: "He doesn't pay attention. He doesn't hand in most of his homework. He bothers the other students when they're working. He's not organized. He rushes through his tests."

As she listens, Charlie's already anxious mother becomes even more anxious. If she's feeling angry at Charlie, she may chime in with her own complaints: "He's just the same way at home. His room is a mess. He won't do his chores unless I nag him." Or she may react defensively and begin blaming the school and the teacher herself: "Well, he had a bad first-grade teacher, and he's never really recovered from that. And he says he's bored in your class. I don't think he's being challenged."

At 4:00 P.M., Mrs. Davis concludes the conference by stating that Charlie will need to work harder or he will be moved to a lower level in reading and math. Mrs. Reimer thanks Mrs. Davis for her time and departs, more confused than ever about what is happening in the class-room and what she can do about it. And she is upset with what she perceives as Mrs. Davis's negative attitude toward her son. Charlie can expect little help to come out of a conference like this.

Constructive parent-teacher conferences take time and preparation. If both parents live in the home, both parents should attend. Joint attendance sends a powerful message to teacher and child alike that both parents are interested and involved. When parents call to schedule a conference, they should ask to meet with all the child's teachers, even those who indicate that the child has "no problems." Some teachers are more hesitant than others to tell parents that their child is having problems because of anxiety about the parents' reaction, because of uncertainty about how to help, or because the child's problems seem insignificant compared with the problems other students in their classes are having. At the middle and high school level, if a youngster is making Cs or Ds, even though she could make As, busy teachers with 120 or so other students may not contact her parents and instead concentrate their efforts on reaching the parents of failing students.

What Not to Talk About

"I'll tell you what the problem is with schools today," intones Mr. Jackson, leaning over the conference table and shaking his finger at the five teachers sitting around it. "The problem with schools today is that they just can't motivate kids!"

A parent-teacher conference is not the place for parents to air their complaints about the child's current teachers, former teachers, the principal, the school, the school system, their own school experiences, American education, or the state of the world. Unfortunately, that is exactly what happens in all too many conferences as teachers' well-meaning comments about the underachiever's problems trigger parents' pent-up anger and anxiety. No child—not the underachiever or her parents before her or any other child—has ever been treated perfectly in school. Educators are human, just as parents are human. If parents need to vent their frustration about unfair treatment they believe their child has received, they should do it somewhere else. Doing so in a conference will only decrease the teacher's security and hamper future treatment efforts.

Nor are conferences the place to confront a spouse over disagreements about how to discipline the child or manage her schoolwork. As a teacher, counselor, and psychologist, I have often seen school conferences deteriorate into an argument between husband and wife over who is to blame for the child's problems. Teachers are not marriage counselors. Confrontations between spouses intimidate teachers and make them less, not more, psychologically available to the parents or child. Instead, parents should try to talk through their painful feelings about the child's problems with each other *before* they go to the school.

What to Talk About

Parents should begin by expressing appreciation for the teacher's time and stating their goals for the conference:

> *"Miss Benton, we really appreciate your taking time to meet with us today. We have some concerns about Jimmy's academic performance and would like to get some help from you in understanding his current achievement and behavior."*

Unfortunately, some teachers react to parents' requests for information with responses designed to placate rather than inform:

> *"Eddie's a darling little boy. He's just immature and needs time to settle down."*

> *"Oh, there's nothing to worry about at all. Anna's still adjusting to third grade."*

Others offer vague generalities rather than specific facts about the child's school progress:

"Sissy isn't really ready for fourth grade. She's so disorganized."

"David doesn't seem to care about his work. I'm afraid he's more interested in socializing than biology."

For these reasons, parents should be prepared with a list of specific questions that will help them determine the child's level of academic performance and effort.

1. In what subjects is the child making good progress and in what subjects does she need help?

2. How often is homework given and in what subjects?

3. For elementary and middle school students, what level is the child's reading group compared with the rest of the class (remedial, average, or advanced), and what is the reading level of the textbook used in her group? Asking about reading levels is important because the child's report card may not indicate the exact grade level at which she is working in favor of more general terms such as *BGL* (below grade level), *R* (remedial), or *D* (developmental), which can mean anything from six months to two or more years below the child's actual grade placement. For example, the average child in the first month of third grade reads at a 3.1 level (third grade, first month). A third grader in the first month of school who is reading at a 2.2 level (second grade, second month) is nearly a year behind her grade peers.

4. Are the students grouped for mathematics, and if so, what level is the child working on and what is the grade level of her math textbook?

5. Are grades assigned by a uniform standard for all students in the school, by a standard for the class, or on an individual ba-

sis? Grading policies vary widely, especially in elementary schools, where teachers may give good grades for effort, regardless of the child's actual achievement level. Thus a child who is working at an average or remedial instructional level may be awarded As if the teacher believes that she is doing the best she can at that level. If parents do not ask about the child's relative standing in her class and grade, they have no way of knowing that the child's good grades do not reflect satisfactory achievement.

In addition to these general questions, parents should ask the following ten questions that are designed specifically to help identify underachievers.

1. Does the child ask for help in ineffective ways, either by asking too often or by not asking for help when she needs it?

2. Does she have trouble completing work, especially when she has to do so on her own?

3. Does she work well when the teacher is near her and shut down when he moves away?

4. Does she give up easily on new or challenging tasks?

5. If she is inattentive, distractible, or impulsive in class, does such behavior increase when she is working independently or is confronted with a difficult task?

6. Does she interpret feedback about her academic work or behavior as criticism and have trouble using feedback to improve her performance?

7. Does she have trouble getting started on and completing long-term projects and written assignments?

8. Does she often forget her school materials, such as paper, pencils, and textbooks?

9. Does she often fail to hand in homework?

10. Does she appear capable of doing better work in class?

Yes answers to three or more of these ten questions indicate a mild underachievement problem. Positive responses to five questions indicate a moderate underachievement problem, whereas positive answers to more than five questions indicate that a severe underachievement pattern exists.

OBTAINING A PSYCHOLOGICAL EVALUATION

If the parents' own assessment and conferences with the teacher indicate that the child is underachieving, parents may wish to request that he receive a psychological evaluation to help identify his academic strengths and weaknesses and determine if he is eligible for services through some special education program. Parents seeking a school-based assessment should bear in mind that obtaining a psychological evaluation for a child is a cumbersome and lengthy process. Because so many children in today's public schools exhibit learning and behavior problems, there is intense competition for special services and for the individual testing that is required by the eligibility and placement process. The child must first be referred to a school-based screening committee, usually consisting of the principal or vice-principal, school psychologist, school social worker, a special education teacher or special education coordinator, and sometimes the guidance counselor. Although the majority of referrals for psychological evaluations are made by classroom teachers, any adult, including parents and other relatives, can request that a child be referred for consideration. The individual requesting the evaluation must complete a form documenting the reasons for the referral, the child's strengths and weaknesses, and interventions that have previously been attempted. A classroom observation by a school staff member, such as the counselor or special education teacher, usually accompanies the referral. If the screening committee believes that other strategies should be tried before testing or that the child may not qualify for any special education services, the request for evaluation may be delayed or denied. In actual practice, however, school personnel generally accede to a parent's request for testing, even if they privately believe that nothing will come of it.

Four kinds of assessments make up the typical school-based evaluation: a battery of individual psychological tests, an educational evaluation, a developmental history, and a medical examination. Psychological testing may be conducted entirely by the school psychologist or shared between the psychologist and an educational testing specialist, often the learning disabilities teacher. Typically, the psychological testing component includes an IQ test, a test of visual-motor functioning, and several personality tests to help determine whether emotional problems are contributing to the child's difficulties in school. The parents and teachers may also be asked to complete rating scales assessing the child's behavior at home and school, especially if the child is suspected of having Attention-Deficit/Hyperactivity Disorder.

The educational assessment may be administered by the school psychologist, educational specialist, or learning disabilities teacher. This component consists of a review of the child's educational history, including attendance, previous grades, and scores from group-administered standardized tests. It also includes one or more achievement tests assessing reading, mathematics, written language, and other important academic skills. Tests to pinpoint specific learning problems, such as diagnostic reading and mathematics tests, may also be included. The child's scores on the achievement tests can then be compared with his scores on the IQ test to determine whether there is a significant discrepancy between his ability and his achievement, the chief criterion for a diagnosis of learning disabilities.

The child's developmental history is taken by a school social worker, who meets with the parents. In addition to taking a detailed history of the child's physical and social development, the social worker asks questions about siblings' adjustment, parent-child interactions, medical or psychiatric problems, and past and current stresses operating in the family. The parents may also be asked to take the child to a physician for a medical evaluation to rule out physical causes for his school problems, or an examination may be provided through the school system.

LIMITATIONS OF PSYCHOLOGICAL EVALUATIONS

After all the assessments have been completed, the school's eligibility committee considers the results and declares that the child either qualifies or does not qualify for special education services, which include services for the mentally retarded (MR), emotionally disturbed (ED), or learning disabled (LD). If the child is declared eligible for one of these categories, the parents must give their permission for him to receive that type of assistance. If the parents are not satisfied with the results of the school-based evaluation, they have the right to obtain a second evaluation by an outside clinician at their own expense. If the child is not found eligible for any special services or the parents disagree with the nature or the amount of the services that are recommended, they also have the right to appeal that decision to a review committee within the school division.

Unfortunately, for most underachievers, school-based psychological evaluations are of little help in understanding or solving their problems. First, some widely used intelligence tests are loaded with items that assess previously acquired knowledge or school learning rather than reasoning ability. The same factors that have lowered the child's classroom performance (inattention, lack of practice on basic skills, and so forth) may therefore also lower his score on the ability test, reducing or removing any discrepancy between ability and achievement. As a result, the child's scores make it look as if he is achieving at a level commensurate with his intellectual potential. Second, in a one-to-one testing situation, the child may perform very differently than he does in the classroom. Indeed, the underachiever is characterized by his lack of effort when he has to work alone, a situation that never occurs in the course of a psychological evaluation.

In addition, the referral and testing process can be agonizingly slow. Because so many children are referred for individual school assessments, delays of months between the initial referral and the final meeting to discuss the results are the rule rather than the exception. It is not uncommon for a child referred in the fall to wait until the spring of the following year to be tested, much less receive some kind of special assistance. Much precious time can be wasted while parents wait for the evaluation process to be completed in the vain hope that somehow testing will reveal the source and the solution of the child's problems.

The Nothing Diagnosis

Mrs. Gadston, the school psychologist, shook her head regretfully as she studied the test scores in front of her. "I'm afraid Barney is one of those 'nothing' kids," she said. "I know he's on the verge of failing fourth grade, but his scores don't qualify him for any kind of special help."

For the vast majority of underachievers who receive a school-based evaluation, the results of testing do not reveal any learning disabilities or emotional problems that can justify placement in a program for the learning disabled or emotionally disturbed. Typically, the special education committee concludes that motivational rather than learning problems are the cause of the child's poor achievement and that he does not fit into any of the available special education programs. School personnel sometimes refer to children who do not conform to the three special education categories (learning disabilities, emotional disturbance, and mental retardation) as the "nothing children," signifying that nothing is wrong with them in terms of the disorders that qualify for federally funded programs.

Alas, when the child is deemed ineligible for placement in a special program, he and his parents are once again left with no solution to his problems. After the long, stressful process of obtaining an evaluation, the parents are told that the child does not fit a category that entitles him to receive special help. When, as often happens, testing indicates that the child is of average or above-average intelligence, has low self-esteem, and is achieving below the level that would be expected based on his ability, that is news to no one. Although the child has been spared an inaccurate label and an inappropriate special education placement, often no alternative treatment is offered. The effect is to tell the parents and the child that there is something wrong with him, but that nobody seems to know exactly what it is and there is no help available for it anyway. Fortunately, however, parents can do much to assist the underachiever and to support school personnel in doing the same. The remainder of this book is devoted to helping them do just that.

Part Two

The World
of the
Underachiever

3.

The Internal World of the Underachiever

To the parents, their child's underachievement is a mystery. Why does their bright child perform so poorly in school? In contrast, the solution to his academic problems seems simple and straightforward: If he would just try harder, he would do better. But this solution fails to work because while it takes into account the underachiever's external behavior (he isn't doing his work), it fails to take into account the internal world that shapes the way in which he interprets and responds to his school experiences.

As is true for all human beings, the underachiever's thoughts, attitudes, and feelings derive from an internal world made up of working models that are to a large extent constructed in infancy and early childhood. These internal images of the self and others constitute a private reality that operates outside the rules of rationality and that corresponds more or less accurately to what is actually happening in the environment. Although the working models of most individuals are flexible enough to allow them to modify their views of themselves and others to match their new experiences, the underachiever's self- and other-models are associated with rigid, maladaptive beliefs that persist in the face of his changing external circumstances. It is the operation of these ineffective internal beliefs that makes so many of his behaviors mysterious and frustrating to his parents and teachers. When the underachiever's apparently irrational behaviors are interpreted from his internal perspective, however, they become much less a mystery than they first appear. In fact, they make excellent sense as far as he is concerned. More important, once understood, the underachiever's maladaptive beliefs and his self-defeating behaviors based on those beliefs become open to change.

BELIEF 1:
I HAVE NO CONTROL OVER
WHAT HAPPENS TO ME

Asked to draw a picture of himself in his sixth-grade classroom, Kevin sketches a group of stick figures with "balloons" enclosing their words. The frowning teacher is standing at the front of the room and commanding, "Class, pass in your papers!" Kevin portrays himself slumped in his chair, while over his head hangs the plaintive message, "But I haven't finished yet." The boy seated behind Kevin is throwing a paper airplane at him, while the girl in front of him turns toward him and demands, "Where's your paper?" The faces of the teacher and students are angry and threatening. His drawing is a vivid portrait of a helpless youngster assaulted by terrifying forces beyond his control.

One of the most striking—and frustrating—characteristics of the underachiever is his failure to take responsibility for his own behavior. He behaves as if his own actions have nothing to do with what happens to him. His persistent refusal to accept responsibility for himself not only prevents him from achieving but also alienates those who are trying to help him, because they perceive his behavior as laziness, obstinacy, or both.

The underachiever's failure to assume responsibility arises from his unconscious belief that his own efforts do not affect the events or individuals in his world, a belief derived from his early experience. If the child's efforts to achieve security and to explore his world are acknowledged and validated by the parent, he develops a sense of self-efficacy. But if his efforts to find a secure base or to explore beyond it are often ignored, discouraged, or modified to meet the parent's needs rather than his own, the child comes to believe that it does not matter what he does. Because from his perspective, his actions do not make a difference, it is logical for him to disavow responsibility for events in the outer world, including his own behavior. Instead, he assigns responsibility to persons or events outside himself.

The underachiever's belief that he lacks control over external events has profoundly negative consequences for his school performance. It does not, for example, make sense for him to pay attention, do homework, or study for tests because those actions will not ultimately have an effect on his grades. He believes that his grades are dependent upon forces in the environment, such as the whims of his teachers or his own good or poor luck at the time. Or he may assign his fate to unknown powers that dictate his competence or incompetence in various subjects: "I'm just no good at science." His parents' efforts to coax, reason, or nag him into trying harder are therefore strenuously resisted. Even when he *tries* to try harder, he privately maintains his belief in his lack of self-efficacy and unconsciously behaves in such a way as to obtain the results he expects.

"I studied for my geography test and I still flunked!" complained Pete, angrily throwing himself into a chair in my office. "I told you it doesn't matter if I study or not!"

Such a youngster firmly believes, first, that he really studied, and second, that his studying did not make a difference. It is pointless for his parents to suggest that he might not have studied effectively or that he might have sabotaged himself on the test by failing to read the directions, neglecting to check his answers, or using a similar strategy from his repertoire of self-defeating behaviors. All he can see is that his attempts to affect his own progress have once again had the negative outcome that he anticipated.

LACK OF CONTROL AND DISORGANIZATION

The underachiever's belief that he has no control over what happens to him is also manifested in a characteristic behavior that drives his parents and teachers to distraction: disorganization. If he spends most of his time at one desk, as in the elementary grades, it is crammed with stubs of pencils, wads of partially completed papers, mangled notebooks, gum wrappers, and broken crayons. By the end of the day, this disorganization has extended to the area around him, so that his desk is encircled with litter.

"As soon as I walked in the classroom, I knew exactly which one was Andy's desk," said his mother ruefully. "It looks just like his room does at home."

Middle and high school underachievers, who change classes each period, keep their lockers in a similar condition. After the first few weeks of school, their lockers are so stuffed with trash that many underachievers simply abandon their lockers and carry all of their books from class to class for the rest of the year. Since, to the underachiever's mind, keeping his materials organized will ultimately have no effect on his performance, it makes much more sense to stuff papers into his notebooks, desks, or lockers than to take time to organize them. Periodic trips to school by his parents to wade through his desks and locker in search of missing papers or in an attempt to restore some semblance of order have only short-term effects. And alas, this intrusion further reinforces the underachiever's conviction that his own actions (even if those actions consist of cramming his materials into his desk or locker) make no difference.

The Catastrophe Around the Corner

The underachiever's belief that there is no connection between his actions and the outcome of those actions also leads him to distrust any success he may enjoy and to anticipate disaster at any moment. His sense of personal incompetence is so entrenched that even success cannot alter his belief that he is incapable of exerting control over his environment. If he does well on a test, he attributes his performance to luck ("The teacher asked the stuff I knew") or innate ability ("I'm smart in math"), rather than to his own efforts ("I studied hard"). Because his internal working models tell him that the connection between persistence and success is unpredictable at best, attempts to convince him that studying made a difference are futile. Thus, parental efforts to encourage him by reminding him that he did well on previous tasks go unheeded. Although he reviews past failures over and over in his thoughts, he ignores past successes. Catastrophe always lurks just around the corner.

In addition, because the underachiever has so few positive psychological supplies upon which to draw, he is highly vulnerable to even the mildest stress. The tensions involved in coping with the daily school routine, especially the demands for independent work, put a constant strain on his limited resources. Because he believes that he can control neither his own actions nor the actions of others, he has no protection against adversity and expends much of his energy fearfully anticipating negative events. Small wonder that he has so much trouble sustaining effort on his classroom and homework assignments.

Failure to Anticipate Consequences

Parents often note that despite the underachiever's obvious intelligence, he seems to have little practical sense and tends to be involved in one disaster after another, ranging from mild social or academic blunders to potentially life-threatening situations. They fail to understand that thinking through the consequences of one's behavior before acting makes sense only if one's behavior *has* consequences. Because the underachiever has internalized the belief that his actions are not predictably related to what happens to him, there is no reason for him to believe that at this particular time, that particular negative outcome will occur. He is therefore shocked when his impulsive behavior results in academic or personal difficulties.

> Troy sat with his hands folded across his chest and a defiant expression on his face. "What did you think was going to happen when you balled up your test paper and threw it in the trash can in front of Miss Willmot?" I asked.
>
> A confused look came over his face. "I don't know," he mumbled. "I guess I didn't think about that."

The underachiever also has great difficulty understanding that events fit logically together to make a final outcome—that is, that the accumulated *total* of behavior, not just one isolated act, determines the course of events. "But I tried *today*," he wails. He is unable to make a connection between the present result (an F for the marking period) and the previous behaviors that contributed to it (an entire six-week period of not paying attention and not doing homework). In schools where warning notices are given midway through the grading period to students with low marks, the underachiever is unable to use the knowledge that he is going to earn a poor grade on his report card if he does not change his behavior. Confronted with the consequences of his failure to heed the warnings, he protests that his final grade is unfair: "Ms. Jennings just doesn't like me!"

Persistence Doesn't Pay

"Jamal's teacher tells us he won't keep trying if something is hard for him. We know what she means because we see the same thing at home," said Jamal's father, sighing. "He'll start building an airplane model and part of the way into it, something won't go quite right, and he'll give up. Sometimes he gets so upset he smashes it."

The securely attached child has learned through repeated experiences that when he needs help, his parent will respond promptly and sensitively to those needs. As a result, he has internalized a competent self-model and an encouraging, helpful model of others. When in the course of his exploration he encounters something new or difficult, he calmly examines the obstacles that stand in the way of his solving the problem, devises strategies for overcoming them, and continues to try, secure in the belief that his persistence will ultimately be rewarded.

In contrast, when the insecurely attached child encountered a challenging situation, his parent responded inconsistently to his efforts to obtain help or responded in ways that heightened rather than reduced his anxiety. Perhaps the parent took over the situation and solved the problem rather than supporting the child's efforts to solve it for himself.

Or the parent might have been so preoccupied with her own worries that she did not respond to his bids for help at all. Now, persisting in the face of difficulty evokes not a model of a parent that encourages effort but a model of a parent imbued with negative and conflictual feelings. To prevent the arousal of these disorganizing emotions, the child's best strategy is either to venture only into areas where he can be highly successful, insuring pleasurable feelings, or to make a brief effort and then give up if things do not work out perfectly at once. For the underachiever, persistence doesn't pay.

Moreover, because the underachiever lacks the inner sustenance afforded by positive models of self and others, he is dependent on outside sources for his motivational fuel. As long as an approving attachment figure is in the immediate vicinity, he may be able to ward off his anxiety and persist with a task. But because his early attempts to master his environment were inconsistently validated, he is unable to incorporate that approval into his self-image and increase his feelings of competency. In fact, he distrusts praise because deep down, he "knows" that he is unlovable and inadequate.

A vicious circle of lack of persistence and failure is thus established. Because his first priority is maintaining the repression of his painful unconscious feelings, he never has the opportunity to persist and discover that persistence pays or to fail and discover that he can learn from his mistakes. In addition, by venturing only into areas where he feels competent, he fails to acquire new skills and problem-solving strategies, thus compounding his academic handicaps. As school progresses, he gradually restricts his sphere of functioning more and more until he is excluding major portions of the curriculum.

BELIEF 2:
I NEED TO BE RESCUED,
BUT I CAN'T BE SAVED

His unfinished papers strewn across his desk, Randy stares at the intercom speaker above the chalkboard in his second-grade classroom for so long that his teacher walks over and asks him what he is looking at.

"I'm waiting," he explains, "for them to call me on the loudspeaker and tell me my mother's come to take me home."

The underachiever's belief that he must rely on someone or something outside himself to solve his predicament arises from several factors related to his internalized models. First, he views himself as an incompetent individual who is incapable of acting in his own behalf. Because during his early development, his efforts at self-direction were ignored, diverted, or discouraged, he does not trust that his own actions will be successful in solving his problems. From his perspective, a magical rescue by some external person or event is his only hope.

Second, his unsatisfied longing for the security afforded by a reliably responsive attachment figure keeps him searching for someone or something that will at last meet that need. All of us indulge from time to time in fantasies of a magical rescue from a pressing problem. ("Maybe somebody will volunteer to take over this project that I can't find the time to do." "Maybe I'll win the lottery so I can pay off my credit card bills.") Most of us recognize, however, that such a rescue will not be forthcoming, and while we may wish for it, we continue trying to solve our own problems. But the underachiever's wish for rescue persists, stifling his efforts to help himself or to use the realistic help offered by his parents and teachers.

The Retreat into Fantasy

In the classroom, where his tasks serve not as opportunities for increasing his sense of mastery but as reminders of his deficiencies, the underachiever defends against his feelings of inadequacy by withdrawing into fantasy, producing the gazing-into-space behavior so often noted by teachers. For young underachievers like Randy, such fantasies usually involve a physical rescue from the drudgery of classroom tasks. They may envision mother coming to school to take them home or the effect of that rescue—playing at home, with mother's presence implied rather than expressed directly in the fantasy.

"I think about my mother and me doing something fun together at home." (first-grade girl)

"I think about staying home. I want to go out in a thunderstorm and get real sick so I can stay home a long time." (second-grade boy)

At first glance, older underachievers' fantasies of rescue appear quite different from those expressed by their younger counterparts. Rather than centering on themes of reunion with mother, they typically feature being with a sweetheart or performing for an admiring audience. Nevertheless, the theme of finding a relationship or scenario that can at last meet their needs for intimacy and validation is identical.

"I think about what it'd be like to have a girlfriend of my own and just be with her a lot." (ninth-grade boy)

"I think about playing my guitar and it's sounding better than it's ever sounded before and the crowd's going wild." (eleventh-grade boy)

The Misinterpretation of Help

Simultaneously existing with the underachiever's unconscious belief that he must await rescue from his problems through an outside agent is his conviction that help will never arrive. This belief is based on his inner model of himself as someone who is not only unable to help himself but is unworthy of being helped by anyone else. In addition, he is suspicious of overtures of help because he has internalized a model of attachment figures who give to him on the basis not so much of his needs as of their own. To make the individuals in his external world conform to his internal representations of unreliable, unhelpful others, the underachiever must distort reality. There are, in fact, people around him who are trying to assist him, but he misinterprets their attempts to help as inappropriate or inadequate. Not only does he misinterpret their positive efforts, he focuses excessively on the negative aspects of his interactions with others at home and school. His parents' many attempts to help him with his homework are forgotten, whereas the one occasion when they decline to take him to the library Sunday night for a book report due on Monday provokes the cry, "You just *want* me to fail!" Similarly, the many times the teacher has patiently answered his questions and given him individual assistance are forgotten. What he remembers and complains about is the one time the teacher failed to come to his aid.

It is important to bear in mind that internalized working models not only shape a person's perceptions, they also lead him to arrange situations in which his expectations are likely to be realized, even if the consequences are painful to him. Thus the underachiever's expectation that he will not be helped causes him unconsciously to induce unhelpful responses in others. At school, he lets the teacher know thirty minutes after a test has begun that he forgot to bring something to write with. Or he displays such a petulant or hostile attitude that his teacher finds interacting with him unpleasant and reduces her efforts to help him. At home, he announces to his parents at 9:00 P.M. that he has a project due the following day—and none of the materials at hand. When he asks for help with homework, he does so in such a way that he invariably evokes a negative response, as he alternately whines about how much work he has, proclaims that he doesn't understand *anything*, and then rejects the help his long-suffering parents offer. An interactional pattern becomes established in which the underachiever makes an ineffective bid for assistance, his parents try to help, he rejects their efforts, and his frustrated parents abandon their attempt to help, thus reinforcing his maladaptive belief system.

> *"Whenever I try to help Stanley with his math, he gets mad and says I don't explain it the way the teacher does," said his father regretfully. "I just can't seem to help him without both of us getting angry."*

TOO LATE FOR HELP

In part, the underachiever rejects the help he so desperately desires because, from his perspective, the time when real help could have been given has passed. Regardless of when or how much help is offered, he believes that it is already too late for him to be saved. This holds true whether he is a second grader or a tenth grader and whether help is offered early or late in the school year. After only one report card, the underachiever is firmly convinced that everything is over and there is nothing he or anyone else can do to change his fate. A chronic underachiever may write off a class after a single poor grade. Convinced that he is going to fail, he behaves in such a way that he fulfills his expectations. "It's too late!" he tells his parents. "There's nothing I can do now." And he proceeds to do just that.

Why does the underachiever act as if his chances of being helped have passed? It is as if he unconsciously recognizes that the true source of his problems lies not in the here and now but in ancient deficits that present-day efforts have no power to remedy. At times, his conviction that current efforts to help him are of no avail gives rise to the fantasy of a magical rebirth into a better existence.

> *"I've really messed up things in school," lamented Evan, laying his head dejectedly on the table. "I wish I could go away somehow and come back again. Then I could start third grade all over again and do it right this time."*

THE WRONG KIND OF HELP

The underachiever's rejection of assistance is also derived from the disparity between help as her parents and teachers perceive it and help as she unconsciously pictures it. The rescue she unconsciously envisions has nothing to do with the realistic assistance with classwork and homework offered by her teachers and parents. The help that she yearns for is a rescue from her painful feelings about herself, her attachment figures, and the struggle of growing up. Because all development entails some form of loss as the individual proceeds from one stage to another, growing up is difficult enough for a child whose attachment and exploratory needs have been adequately met. But the insecurely attached child remains paralyzed at the threshold of her own life, trapped between her drive to explore independently and her persistent, unmet needs for security and validation. Unconsciously, she longs to be rescued not by her parents or teachers but by the mother of her infancy, who, in her fantasy, is now wholly available and responsive. Although she has no real expectation that this mother will come, she is unable to give up her fantasy, accept some other form of assistance in its place, and thus leave childhood forever unsatisfied. So she responds by not asking for help, by ignoring help when it is offered, by first demanding help and then resisting it, or by refusing help in other self-defeating ways.

BELIEF 3:
IF SOMETHING ISN'T PERFECT,
IT'S AWFUL

After working for a few minutes on his English assignment, Jerome makes a disgusted face, balls up his paper, and stuffs it in his desk. With a loud sigh, he pulls a fresh sheet of paper out of his notebook and begins writing again. When the bell rings to mark the end of the period, his desk is crammed with crumpled pieces of paper and he has completed less than a third of the assignment.

The underachiever believes that only two alternatives in life are possible: perfection or failure. His splitting of experience into polarities is especially noticeable in his characterizations of others: Parents, depending on what they are doing at that moment, are either gratifying or depriving. Teachers are either helpful or mean. Peers are either supportive or backstabbing. Why does the underachiever have such difficulty conceiving of a middle ground?

All children have a tendency to categorize their experience as black and white, good and bad, a tendency that diminishes as they become mature enough to integrate the positive and negative aspects of individuals and events into realistic representations. But because many of his early experiences met with inconsistent or insensitive responding, the underachiever has internalized a model of the self endowed with feelings of inferiority and damage. To defend against these painful feelings, the underachiever sets up perfectionistic standards for himself, believing unconsciously that only a perfect performance will compensate for his inadequacy and earn him the closeness and validation he has so long been seeking.

Over time, setting lofty goals becomes reinforcing because it helps to counter his feelings of vulnerability. Moreover, by selecting grandiose, unattainable goals for himself, the underachiever can preserve his secret fantasy that he is superior to those around them. The *thought* of the perfect assignment compensates, at least partially, for the completed work. Perfectionistic goal setting also provides the underachiever with an illusory sense of control over his own actions: "If I wanted to, I could do it," he tells himself and others. "I just don't want to."

The Effects of Perfectionism on Achievement

Tragically, the underachiever's belief that only perfection can compensate for her inferiority further inhibits her productivity. Her grandiose goals fail to promote achievement because they are conceived not as guides for directing her present actions but as guides for actions that will occur some time in the future. Instead of telling herself, "I'll study hard for my physics test this Friday," the underachiever tells herself, "I'll turn everything around the next marking period." Or, "If I make it to seventh grade, I'll be a straight-A student." A goal to guide her present behavior would pose too great a threat to her defenses.

The underachiever's perfectionistic goals also undermine her efforts to improve because they focus on the product rather than the process of learning. The underachiever does not say to herself, "I'll spend twenty minutes studying my vocabulary words tonight." Instead, she conceives of her goal in terms of the *product* of studying: "I'm going to get an A on my vocabulary test." Although her emphasis on product is understandable in light of her earlier failure to learn the connection between actions and outcomes, it is counterproductive because it fails to specify the behaviors that will help her change her current situation to what she would like it to be.

Finally, because her lofty goals are designed to counteract her feelings of inferiority rather than serve as guidelines for action, she sets them so much higher than her present level of performance that even beginning to work toward them seems an impossible task. Thus at the same time that they protect her from being overwhelmed by her feelings of inadequacy, they also make it hard for her to take the small steps that would help her start climbing out of the hole she has dug for herself, and she remains paralyzed in a state of inaction. In the end, her failure to attain her perfectionistic goals further confirms her belief in herself as a powerless individual.

> *"Mr. Sanders gave me a D on my lab report,"* reported Gary, slumping down into his chair dejectedly. When I suggested that he still had most of the six weeks to pull up his science grade, he retorted angrily, *"But I wanted to make an A this six weeks, and now it's too late!"*

The Operation of Perfectionistic Thinking in the Classroom

The underachiever's all-or-nothing thinking manifests itself not only in unrealistic goal setting but in other counterproductive classroom behaviors as well. It is particularly apparent in the first stages of a task that must be completed independently. Elementary school underachievers are capable of sitting for inordinate periods of time with their pencils poised over their blank paper before beginning to create vocabulary sentences or copy a brief paragraph from the chalkboard. Older underachievers are often so overwhelmed by the many choices confronting them in a creative writing assignment or long-term project that they never get to the task itself. When confronted by their parents or teacher with their failure to complete the assignment, they protest, "But I just couldn't think of what to write about!"

The underachiever's belief that only perfection can rescue his damaged self interferes severely with his performance on tests. Halfway through a test, the underachiever discovers some mistake, typically the result of not following directions, and becomes either so anxious that he can't concentrate on the rest of the test or so furious that he shuts down completely. Reworking the paper is not considered. One mistake means that the paper is "*all* messed up" or that he has "ruined *everything.*" Less than perfect is the same as a zero. The test anxiety that is often cited as a contributing factor to underachievement is a misnomer. What the underachiever fears is not the testing situation but the disorganizing anxiety that threatens to be aroused if his performance does not meet his own perfectionistic standards.

PERFECTIONISM AND ENTITLEMENT

For a sizable number of underachievers, their perfectionistic beliefs are buttressed by feelings of entitlement. These youngsters are beset with such painful feelings of inadequacy that they ward them off not only by perfectionistic aspirations but also by a defensive overvaluing of the self. Beneath their "I don't care" presentation, they harbor a covert, largely unconscious view of themselves as so superior to others that achievement in the ordinary sense of the word should not be required of them. They believe that they are entitled to special privileges in school, that regular classroom work is beneath them, and that they should be awarded good grades merely for attending class and participating in discussions. They are especially likely to believe that their *selection* of a unique project or an unusual method for carrying out an assignment is equivalent to the *product* itself and should be judged accordingly.

It can be very difficult to detect the operation of these entitled attitudes in the underachiever, as he sits passively in the classroom, an observer rather than a participant in his own learning. Such feelings of superiority often remain beyond the child's own awareness and are seldom expressed outside a therapeutic environment, where the child senses that they will not be criticized.

> *Sixth-grade Lance spent most of his time in class twirling his lanky blond hair in his fingers or looking out the window. Although he did well on tests and participated in discussions that interested him, he completed very little written work. "I know how to do that stuff, and I get tired of doing it," he commented during one counseling session. He paused and then added thoughtfully, "I guess I feel like I shouldn't have to do the things the other kids do."*

BELIEF 4:
GROWING UP DOESN'T GET YOU ANYWHERE

"When I grow up, I'm never going to move away. I'm going to build a house on the hill right next to Mom's house. And I'll help her around the house and yard and we'll live there together forever." (fifth-grade underachiever)

Because the underachiever lacks an internalized model of herself as competent and a model of others as helpful when she is in need, she feels ill-equipped to cope with the challenges of life. Instead of moving outward with a confidence based on an internal image of herself as capable and of others as warmly encouraging her discoveries, she must venture forth on the strength of an internal world peopled by an inadequate self and unreliable attachment figures. At this stage of her development, learning in school, especially independent learning, symbolizes growing up. Because growing up arouses intense anxiety, however, she must devise strategies to avoid independent work and thus avert the dangers she unconsciously fears.

REGRESSIVE BEHAVIOR AS A
DEFENSE AGAINST GROWING UP

The underachiever's fear of growing up is manifested in the regressive behavior he displays at home and at school. Although he may not differ in chronological age from his classmates, he often has less adequate social skills and may appear younger because of his more childish facial expressions and mannerisms. At home and at school, he often seems like a toddler, as he constantly demands attention, clings to his parents and teachers, and then resists their efforts to help him.

Parents and teachers alike often interpret the child's regressive behavior as arising from his being "spoiled" and wishing to be "babied." But the child's clinging and demanding behavior is not the result of his unwillingness to give up the nurturance that the parents *currently* provide. It stems from his unwillingness to abandon the hope that one day he will experience a genuine childhood in which his parents will be able to provide the kind of nurturance and support that they could not provide during his early development. The child of a distant or rejecting parent unconsciously avoids exploring too far from the maternal orbit in the hope that somehow he can coax the parent into becoming warm and responsive. The child whose parent has overly controlled his exploratory efforts also avoids moving away because of his unmet longing for free, self-directed exploration before the eyes of an admiring, encouraging parent. For the child whose parent promoted dependency rather than exploration, independent effort reactivates the implicit threat of abandonment delivered earlier by the parent. Despite the healthy aspect of him that longs to be separate, he cannot risk developing the autonomous behaviors that might prompt the withdrawal of support. He is therefore careful to send out messages that he is immature, irresponsible, and inept. In any case, the child unconsciously clings to childhood by failing to carry out the responsibilities that symbolize growing up, both at home and at school.

Coexisting with the child's fear of growing up, however, is his healthy drive toward higher development. The enticing world beckons, and his natural tendency toward growth yearns to answer that call. The underachiever's struggle to manage his conflicting desires—to grow up and yet to remain a child—finds expression in rapid fluctuations of his behaviors and attitudes. One moment, he is clinging to his parents or teachers, and the next, he is angrily rejecting their help and proclaiming that he can do it on his own. Unaware of the unconscious beliefs underlying these push-pull interactions, the adults trying to assist him become confused and are likely to respond inconsistently themselves.

The underachiever's fear of growing up is most evident as he approaches a transitional point in his education, such as the change from one level of school to another. Although his anxieties seem to be focused on the impending school change, his real fear is of what that transition symbolizes—a step toward a stage of greater independence.

At the age of six, Arnie was one of the brightest children in his first-grade class. Unfortunately, he was so inattentive and distractible that he had fallen behind his classmates and was almost certainly going to be recommended for retention.

"What does the idea of going to second grade make you think of?" I asked him.

"It makes me sick," he responded instantly, making a face.

THE GOLDEN AGE OF ACHIEVEMENT

Underachievers' ambivalence about growing up finds poignant expression in their conviction that somewhere in the past they enjoyed a golden age of achievement, a time when they excelled in school. Accompanying this belief is a profound sense of loss because the golden age of achievement is over and, to their minds, can never be regained, regardless of their efforts. Parents are unlikely to be privy to the underachiever's reminiscences about this golden age because the child fears that his parents will either remind him that he never had such a positive period or become even more disappointed with his poor performance in the present. In the nonevaluative environment of a therapy session, however, underachievers of every age will spontaneously reminisce about a former time when they achieved at a high level. Often this time is remembered as the pinnacle not only of academic achievement but also of social acceptance, a time when they enjoyed great popularity with classmates and teachers alike.

Listening to underachievers talk about this golden age of achievement is very much like hearing elderly persons talking nostalgically about the good old days. The period in school that is remembered as the golden age is related to the age of the underachiever. High school students usually report elementary school as having been positive without referring to a particular grade. Middle school students tend to remember their first two or three grades as "good," whereas for elementary school students, kindergarten is usually the last grade they remember as "fun" or "good."

The underachiever's age is also related to the degree to which he remembers this time in all-positive terms. The younger the child, the more likely he is to describe this golden age in absolutes. He was not just good in school, he was the best. He was not just one of the students who worked quickly, he was the first to finish. The teacher not only enjoyed having him in class, he was her very favorite pupil. Older underachievers use fewer superlatives to describe their performance but still emphasize that school was a much more positive experience than it is currently.

First-grade boy: "In kindergarten, I was always the first one done, and I got to do extra things to help Miss Grady. Not now. Now I don't finish my work."

Fourth-grade girl: "In first grade, I was the smartest one in my class, and the teacher and everybody really liked me. Then everything changed."

Ninth-grade boy: "Back in elementary school, the work seemed fun and really easy. When I got to middle school, school wasn't so much fun anymore and the teachers got meaner. Here in the high school, things are really bad. Nobody knows who you are. I'm never going to make it out of ninth grade."

The description of the golden age of achievement is remarkably similar across sexes, ages, and grades. The key features of the memories are the emphasis on the enjoyable aspects of learning, the special relationship with the teacher, and positive feelings about the self and others. It is as if the underachiever intuitively understands the conditions that foster high achievement. When work is both pleasurable and challenging, a sense of personal competence can develop. Moreover, the memory includes an affectionate bond with the teacher, so that the learning environment provides not only validation for mastery but closeness with an attachment figure as well.

For some underachievers, these reminiscences are at least partially accurate, although colored by time and selective remembering. Over more than a decade in a small school system with a highly stable population, I watched all too many youngsters who displayed considerable academic promise in kindergarten and first grade fail to realize that promise as they progressed through school. For other children, however, these memories are pure fantasies. Always mediocre students, they never enjoyed a golden age of achievement, not even in kindergarten.

Nevertheless, they, too, cherish the belief in a golden age and describe it in the same terms as do other underachievers who have in reality performed at a higher level.

> *Timmy, a severely underachieving second grader who spent most of his time in the classroom staring into space and sucking on his pencil, smiled happily when I asked him how school had been the previous year. "Last year I got all As!" he exclaimed proudly and went on to describe how well he had done his work. A check of his cumulative record revealed that all of his grades for the preceding year had been Cs and Ds.*

What is the meaning of such a belief? Is it a wish-fulfilling fantasy or an outright lie? Underachievers who spin tales of a golden age of achievement are not deliberately lying, even when nothing remotely approaching such an age ever existed in their background. What these children are remembering is the happy, playful atmosphere of the early grades, when there is an emphasis on feeling good about the self as a learner as well as on the development of academic skills. Moreover, teachers in the primary grades tend to be verbally and physically affectionate with their students, creating a warm, secure environment just as a loving mother does for her infant. The positive memories also help protect the underachiever from his feelings of inadequacy. It would be overwhelmingly threatening to his fragile sense of self if he could not look back to at least one period in the past when he had done well in school.

Regardless of whether the golden age of achievement really existed, the underachiever is convinced that good times at school are lost forever. With memories, realistic or fantastic, of a blissful past, he looks out on a present darkened by the cloud of his failure and into a future unlighted by the hope of improvement.

4.

The Underachiever at School

Sam is a seven-year-old second grader. He doesn't pay attention, he rushes through his work, and he pesters his classmates. In his teacher's words, he "buzzes around the room like a bee." His teacher is sick and tired of trying to get him to settle down and do his work. His classmates are sick and tired of his bothering them while they're trying to do their work. His parents are sick and tired of hearing nothing but bad news from the school.

When a child enters school, she carries with her the internalized images of herself and others that she has constructed over the years. Although these internal perspectives are unconscious, they shape her expectations about how successful she will be as a student. They also guide her interactions with her teachers and peers, based on what she has come to believe about how other people will act toward her. In fact, she tends to induce her teachers and classmates to behave the way that her internal views of others tell her to expect. Depending on the nature of her internal beliefs, her school experiences may arouse positive feelings that encourage learning, negative feelings that discourage it, or ambivalent feelings that make learning desirable but dangerous.

Although the child's internal images of herself and others are chiefly constructed during early development, they continue to be modified by the way in which the major figures in her life at home and school interact with her. When her parents and teachers are able to communicate their belief in her value as a person and encouragement for her efforts to master her academic tasks, adaptive images can be strengthened and maladaptive images can be modified in more positive directions. But when, despite her parents' and teachers' conscious intentions, they communicate a lack of belief in the child's worth, a lack of support for her efforts, or both, effective images can be eroded and ineffective images can be reinforced.

THE PARENTS' INTERPRETATION OF SCHOOL

"Mom, can you help me with my lab report?" Report in hand, Bonnie pops her head into her mother's bedroom, where her mother is making the bed.

"Oh, sweetie, I was never any good at science," her mother answers hastily. "You'll have to wait till your father gets home and ask him. But if you need any help with English, let me know."

With a sigh, Bonnie goes back to her bedroom and sits down at her desk. But she does not continue working on her lab report. Instead, she puts it aside, turns on her desk radio, and picks up her English book.

Just as in his early development, the child monitored his parents' reactions to help determine his feelings about exploration, so he now continues to assess his parents' responses to his educational experiences. From the moment that school is first mentioned in the household, to the child's entry into preschool, through high school and college, parents are constantly sending out conscious and unconscious signals that shape the manner in which the child approaches and evaluates his life at school. Do his parents seem pleased or anxious about his efforts to master his academic work? Do they enthusiastically validate his small successes, or do they tell him he can do better? Are they interested in what he is learning and how he feels about learning, or do they seem to be more interested in his grades? When he asks for help, do they provide him with just enough help to get him going again, or do they take over his assignments and end up helping too much? Each parent-child interaction modifies the internal perspectives that guide the child's attitudes toward learning.

THE INFLUENCE OF PARENTS' MEMORIES AND FEELINGS ABOUT SCHOOL

"I used to think going to college would be kind of cool," recalled Brad, who was coasting through tenth grade with Cs and Ds. "But Dad keeps going on and on about how hard he had to study in college and how I've got to get into the right school and take the right kind of program, and it just sounds like more work. Sometimes I don't even think I want to go to college. I'm sick of studying as it is!"

When parents have had generally positive school experiences or when they are able to acknowledge and work through their negative school experiences, they can help their child view school as a place where he can feel secure and explore freely. Such parents provide support for the child's efforts and share enthusiastically in his daily school experiences. Moreover, they encourage him to use his teachers as resources and to form relationships with his classmates, further enhancing the security of school as a base. As the child encounters new academic and social challenges, he moves forward with confidence, secure within an ever-expanding network of reliable, helpful people.

But for parents who have been unable to work through negative feelings about their own school years, the child's academic experiences trigger troubling memories and emotions. Every single one of the hundreds of parents of underachievers I've worked with over the years has had some kind of unhappy school experience. Parents may have painful memories associated with certain grades, teachers, subjects, or school situations, such as taking tests or performing in front of their classmates. But the feelings and memories that are most likely to interfere with their efforts to encourage their child's achievement are related to their own parents' interactions with them about school. As the child progresses through school, his experiences reactivate those disturbing memories and feelings. To ward off their painful emotions, parents may try to deny them.

"I know I don't have much time to pay attention to Steven's homework. My dad never had time to hear about my day at school either," commented Mr. Anderson, the father of an underachieving fourth grader. "But, hey, that's how life was back then. He was busy all the time and didn't want to be bothered. It didn't make any difference to me."

Others attempt to cope with their disturbing memories by sharing them with the child.

"Now, Martha, honey, I know just how you feel about this terrible algebra," said her mother soothingly. "I never understood anything about those xs and ys either. When I was your age, I can remember going home and crying after every algebra test."

Although it is not necessarily inappropriate for parents to share their negative school experiences with their child, it can be difficult to do so in ways that are encouraging rather than discouraging to the child. Such messages as "I couldn't do spelling either" or "I never got along with my teachers" may seem supportive of the child's struggles, but they make it more, not less, difficult for him to behave effectively because he senses the painful feelings his efforts evoke in his parents. Unfortunately, some parents burden the child with their own emotional baggage about school by talking about their disappointing experiences without also telling the child how they coped with their problems. Listening to such a recitation of woes, the child is likely to feel guilty if his school experiences are more positive than those of his parents. As a result, he may unconsciously undermine his own performance in an attempt to avoid contributing to their distress.

School as a Loss for the Insecure Parent

The advent of school creates a regular and permanent separation in the parent-child relationship and introduces a multiplicity of competing influences for the child's attention and interest. Most parents welcome this opportunity for their child to increase his competency by exploring other worlds and other relationships. But the parent whose own family was unable to meet her needs for security is likely to react with anxiety to the child's growing autonomy and to communicate messages that foster his continuing dependence on her. It is not so much what she *tells* the child about school as her unconscious emotional response to his efforts to move beyond the maternal orbit that affects his attitudes toward school.

Struggling with so many unmet needs of her own, the insecure parent has come to rely on the child as a source of comfort for herself. His entry into school threatens her psychological equilibrium because it threatens to disrupt their overly involved relationship. Such a parent cannot present school to the child as a secure base outside the family. Unconsciously, she fears his investment in his schoolwork, teachers, and classmates because she sees that investment as diminishing rather than enriching their relationship. She therefore interprets school to the child not as an exciting place full of challenges for him to meet and master but as a place *where she is not*. Even if she tries to display a positive attitude toward school, the child is not deceived. As with all parent-child communications, the child can readily sense when the conscious, spoken message differs from the unconscious, unspoken message. The mother who tells the child, "Don't worry, you'll do fine at school," but says it with an anxious expression convinces neither herself nor the child that school is a safe environment within which he will be a happy, competent learner. As a result, even when he enjoys his teachers, classmates, and activities, his learning is never wholly free of anxiety.

> *Six-year-old Jerry's parents had recently separated, and his mother was working as a cook in a local restaurant. He came right to the point in explaining the reasons for his poor performance in first grade. "I can't do my work because I worry about Mom. I worry that there might be a fire at the restaurant and she might get burned."*

For her part, the insecure parent may intensify the child's fears by suggesting to him that something will happen to her while the two are separated. Although consciously she does not mean to distress the child, her own anxiety at the threatened loss of her major source of self-esteem is so great that unconsciously she fosters his concern.

Jerry's mother also had no difficulty in tracing the source of her son's fears. "I know he worries about me when I'm at work," she said with a smile. "He knows how hard I work and how nasty the customers can be sometimes. The other day I told him about how one of the other cooks got badly burned on the stove and now he's afraid I'll get burned, too. I tell him to just forget about me when he's at school, but he still worries."

SCHOOL AS A STAGE FOR THE UNVALIDATED PARENT

When a parent is relying on the child for the validation his own parents could not provide, he, too, cannot communicate to the child that school is a secure base. An individual whose parents were unable to respond with enthusiastic admiration to his budding achievements tends to go through life searching for substitutes to assume that role. As a marital partner and parent, he unconsciously views his spouse and child as extensions of himself rather than as separate individuals with their own interests and needs. The child's school experiences (like all his experiences) are unconsciously viewed as the parent's, not the child's.

For the unvalidated parent, being special (or rather, gaining the recognition from others that comes with being special) is the supreme achievement. When being special is equated with achieving at a high level, the solution can be adaptive, at least temporarily. But because the child is striving to achieve to meet her parent's needs rather than her own, she is an anxious rather than a happy learner. No one, not even the most gifted and industrious child, can always be the best at everything, so the child is perpetually in a state of tension. Ultimately, the child's anxiety may become overwhelming and erupt in the form of misbehavior, withdrawal from competition, or psychosomatic illnesses, especially stomach complaints and eating disorders.

Mrs. Tompkins, the fifth-grade teacher, had a worried look on her face. "I had scheduled a test for this morning," she explained, "and not long after Gail arrived, she was complaining of such severe stomach pains that I sent her to the nurse. Now she swears she wants to take the test, but she looks so ill I don't think she should. What really concerns me is that lately this has been happening every time we have a test."

Gail's stomachaches were so persistent that her parents feared she might be developing an ulcer and took her to a pediatrician, who prescribed antacid medication. As the months went by, the stomachaches became more frequent, and more and more medication was necessary. For Gail, each test brought with it the fear of a less-than-perfect performance—and the fear of disappointing her needy parents.

THE UNDERACHIEVER IN THE CLASSROOM

THE SECURELY ATTACHED CHILD IN THE CLASSROOM

Joseph sits at his desk in his second-grade classroom with his morning seatwork before him. He looks briefly through his reading and arithmetic worksheets before putting them in his desk, placing them carefully on top of his other books so they don't wrinkle. He arranges his writing paper in front of him and examines the paragraph written on the chalkboard. When the teacher calls a group of children back to the reading table, he briefly turns around to watch them take their places but then picks up his pencil and begins copying the paragraph. He works busily, pausing occasionally to study his efforts. After ten minutes, he is finished. "Done!" he whispers to himself and proudly displays his completed paper to one of his classmates before tucking it in his desk and taking out his reading worksheet.

The child who is fortunate enough to possess an image of herself as competent and an image of others as helpful is ready and eager to explore new areas of learning and new relationships at school. Because she is loved for herself rather than for the emotional supplies she provides, she develops the expectation of being valued, regardless of her performance. When confronted with challenging situations, she can draw upon her internalized image of a helpful, approving parent and on the sense of security and encouragement that such a mental image provides. She has an inner secure base that provides the reassurance and motivation that helps her persist, even when her tasks are tedious or difficult. Moreover, because her self-image is of someone who is capable and worthy of being helped, she will actively seek out assistance when she needs it.

THE INSECURELY ATTACHED CHILD IN THE CLASSROOM

But for the child who lacks the internal security afforded by positive views of himself and others, the academic and social challenges of the school day evoke feelings and thoughts that make learning an anxiety-provoking experience. Although his teacher *seems* to be encouraging him to learn, his internal images tell him that he is incapable of doing his work and that she will be unable to help him if he needs her. When he encounters obstacles, as the learning process invariably entails, he has few inner resources on which to draw and little hope of receiving help from anyone else. Even if he could summon the courage to try, the voices of his internal world whisper that it is safer to do nothing or to find something to distract himself from his worries.

Each child's unique early experiences and his internal views of himself and others derived from those experiences are manifested in a unique set of responses to school. In general, however, underachievers' behavior can be classified as belonging to one of four styles. These styles overlap to some extent and by no means exhaust the range of ineffective behaviors that underachievers are capable of displaying in the classroom. Regardless of the differences in their outward appearance, however, all four behavioral styles are based on the operation of maladaptive internal perspectives that are derailing the child's efforts to be a successful student.

The Passive-Avoidant Underachiever

Ms. Cromwell is reading a story to her kindergarten class. Nearly all of the fifteen children seated on the rug are clustered tightly around her, craning their necks for a closer look at the pictures she displays with each turn of the page. Only Lucy hangs back, sitting on the edge of the rug as far away from the teacher as possible. Unlike the other children, she does not look at the teacher as she reads but gazes vacantly around the room or down at her own hands. When the other children exclaim excitedly over a picture, she turns briefly to see but then immediately looks away again.

For the child whose efforts at exploration have often been interrupted, redirected, or criticized, confronting new challenges arouses unpleasant feelings of overstimulation and helplessness. To ward off those painful feelings, she has developed an avoidant approach to experience. Now in the classroom, she either waits for things to happen to her or withdraws to prevent things from happening to her. Moreover, because she believes that she has little influence over the nature and extent of her exploration, she does not actively seek her teacher's help in solving problems. Instead, she passively waits for the teacher to come and guide her throughout the process. Or she may go through the motions of learning, doing just enough to avoid criticism but never fully investing in the task.

The Active-Avoidant Underachiever

In the front row of his third-grade classroom, eight-year-old Donald sits wiggling in his chair, his seatwork piled in front of him. Instead of working, however, he whispers to the boy next to him. Receiving no response, he begins tapping his pencil repeatedly on his desk. Then he leans over to look into the compartment under his chair and remains suspended nearly upside down for a minute. When neither the teacher nor his classmates pay any attention to this maneuver, he falls out of his chair and begins rifling through his materials, noisily pulling out papers, pencils, and books and scattering them on the floor.

"Donald, get back in that chair!" commands his teacher. Donald reluctantly climbs back into his chair, glancing around to see if his classmates are watching him. A second later he bounces up out of his seat again and, catching the eye of a boy on his way to the pencil sharpener at the back of the classroom, races him to it. "I beat!" he proclaims triumphantly, standing in front of the pencil sharpener. Donald continues to block the other boy from using the pencil sharpener, but he does not use it himself because he has not brought his pencil with him.

Like the passive-avoidant underachiever, the active-avoidant under-achiever has come to associate exploration with interruption, redirec-tion, or rejection. Because concentrating on a task now arouses unpleasant, disorganizing feelings, the child has learned to use overac-tivity as a way of detaching himself from the task before the expected disruption can occur. By never persisting with anything very long, he avoids the threat of triggering his painful emotions, but he also prevents himself from investing in and obtaining any real satisfaction from his academic work. Although at first glance, he may appear to be an eager student, now talking to the teacher, now interacting with classmates, now working at his lessons, closer observation reveals that he is not fully engaged in any activity. Because of his failure to pay attention or follow through on tasks, the active-avoidant underachiever is often identified as having Attention-Deficit/Hyperactivity Disorder (ADHD). But his restlessness is not the purposeless hyperactivity of a child with a neuro-logically based disorder. On the contrary, it unconsciously serves the function of warding off his anxiety-provoking feelings.

The Dependent Underachiever

Most of the second graders in Miss Hinkle's classroom have finished copying a paragraph about the Pilgrims' landing at Plymouth Rock and are drawing a picture to illustrate it. Seven-year-old Patrick hums, makes smacking noises, and rocks vigorously in his chair but does not work. Miss Hinkle approaches him. "Patrick, what's your job right now?" she asks.

"Write," he mumbles.

"Good. When you finish copying the paragraph, you can draw the fort and some Indians on your paper."

Patrick begins copying the paragraph from the chalkboard but after only a few minutes, he jumps out of his seat, walks over to Miss Hinkle, and thrusts the paper at her. "This good?" he demands in a babyish tone.

"That's fine. Keep on working," she responds. Patrick returns to his desk, making clicking noises to himself. He works for another two min-utes, still making clicking noises, and then jumps up suddenly and goes over to the teacher again.

"Where's my crayons?" he asks plaintively. Without giving her time to answer, he repeats, "Where's my crayons?"

"Look in your desk," answers the patient Miss Hinkle.

Patrick wanders back to his seat and pulls his books and papers out of his desk and onto the floor. He discovers his box of crayons but instead of writing or drawing, he sits looking at the box, turning it over and over in his hands.

Because his parent was more attentive when he needed comfort and help than when he sought validation for his accomplishments, the dependent underachiever has internalized an image of himself as incompetent and an image of others who respond primarily to his neediness. Because he feels incapable of performing tasks on his own, he demands that his teacher help him with every little thing. Only the teacher's constant attention can relieve the anxiety he associates with exploration to the point where he can do his work. When she moves away, his anxiety becomes so unmanageable that he either shuts down or misbehaves to force her to return to his side. Even her disapproval is preferable to her failure to interact with him at all.

The dependent underachiever not only has trouble beginning and completing his work, he also has trouble sharing materials, taking turns, and working cooperatively with his peers. Such behaviors do not arise out of selfishness but out of a lack of confidence that he will get his fair share. Thus he will demand (or cry or whine or fight) to be first in the lunch line, first to read aloud, and first in games at recess. Over time, his teacher and classmates grow weary of his demanding behavior and begin rejecting him, which only makes him increase his ineffective bids for attention and affection.

The Performance-Oriented Underachiever

"I just have to make an A in math," explained Carrie. "If I don't, it'll kill my father. He's an engineer, and he expects us to be math whizzes just like him." As she spoke, she twirled her hair around and around her fingers, revealing nails bitten down to the quick.

The child of an unvalidated parent, the performance-oriented underachiever has internalized the belief that he is valuable only when he engages in certain kinds of performances or only when his performance reaches a certain standard. When such a child goes to school, he tries desperately to win the approval of the teacher by unique productions or a charming manner. But because he believes that only very special performances will earn him validation, he retreats from situations that challenge his skills. Learning for its own sake has little appeal. Instead, he values learning only as a means of obtaining the approval of others.

Because the performance-oriented underachiever tends to be engaging and highly verbal, his maladaptive behaviors may go unnoticed for some time. But because he must expend so much energy on captivating an uncertain audience, he is unable to reach his full potential. No matter how well he does today, he feels anxious and unfulfilled because his present-day successes cannot guarantee approval from others in the future. Although his anxiety may seem to be focused on tests and other evaluative situations, it is not evaluation itself that arouses his distress. It is the threat that his performance may not be good enough to win the affirmation for which he longs. In the early grades, he may have positive feelings about school, but the evaluation process is so stressful that his ability to invest in learning gradually diminishes. Moreover, although his anxiety may drive him to become temporarily an overachiever rather than an underachiever, his fear of failure is so great that he learns to avoid competing in any areas except those in which he can be highly successful, narrowing his range of choices and ultimately his own development.

How the Underachiever Asks for Help

Most of Mrs. Mayberry's fourth graders are working on their morning seatwork, while she conducts a reading group with five students in the back of the classroom. As Myron encounters a difficult math problem on his paper, he suddenly stops, puts his hand up, and looks around to see where Mrs. Mayberry is. Seeing that she is busy with the reading group, he sighs, puts his hand down, and looks at his paper again. After a moment, he resumes writing.

When a child confronts a challenging task, she automatically and unconsciously consults her internal world to help her decide how to deal with it. She consults her view of herself to ask, "Am I capable of performing this task?" She also checks her view of others to ask, "Will I be able to get help if I need it?" The securely attached child obtains positive answers to both of her questions. Confident that she will be able to master whatever comes her way or will be able to get help if she runs into problems, she proceeds with energy and enthusiasm through her daily assignments.

As long as the insecurely attached child feels capable of successfully completing a task on her own, she looks very much like the securely attached child in the classroom. But when she encounters an obstacle, she evokes internal images of the self and others that interfere with her ability to persist. First, the self-image that she evokes is of someone who is incompetent and unworthy of being helped. Second, the images of others that she evokes are linked with unpredictable or unhelpful responses to her exploratory efforts, as well as the unpleasant emotions associated with those responses. Feeling overwhelmed rather than encouraged, she now wants to check with her teacher, her nearest attachment figure, to help her manage her conflicting feelings. But because she has no real confidence that the teacher will be available to help her, she expresses her bid for help in indirect and ineffective ways.

The way in which the underachiever expresses her wish for help varies according to her behavioral style. The passive-avoidant underachiever sits mutely in her chair and hopes that the teacher will magically read her mind and respond to her unspoken need.

"Please pass up your classwork," instructs Miss Jeffreys. As she collects the papers from her fifth graders, one paper catches her attention.

"Paul, you haven't done any of your math problems!" she exclaims.

"Didn't have a pencil," he mutters.

Miss Jeffreys shakes her head in angry disbelief. "If you didn't have a pencil, why, for goodness' sake, didn't you ask for one?" she asks incredulously.

Paul sinks lower in his seat and does not respond.

The active-avoidant underachiever is also hesitant to approach his teacher and seek help directly. In contrast to the passive-avoidant underachiever, however, he expresses his wish for help through restless, distracting, and impulsive behaviors that are sure to attract attention from the teacher—of a negative kind.

"Bert, I've told you three times to sit down and get to work on your spelling definitions!" exclaims Mr. Tucker, the third-grade language arts teacher. "You spend more time out of your chair than in it!"

Bert returns reluctantly to his seat, where his spelling paper waits unfinished on his desk, and his three table mates are working busily. Bert looks at the directions for the spelling exercise for a moment and then begins spinning his pencil on the table. The boy next to him gives him a baleful look, edges his chair away, and continues working. Bert catches the eye of the girl opposite him and makes a face at her.

"Mr. Tucker, Bert's making faces at me!" she cries.

"Bert, stop bothering Samantha and do your work!" admonishes Mr. Tucker.

When the dependent underachiever wants help from the teacher (which is most of the time), she uses a variety of behaviors that express not only her wish for help but also her anger that the teacher will not assume the responsibility for her learning. Her bids for help, such as dropping her books, sighing loudly, or getting up frequently to sharpen her pencils, have a petulant quality to them. Not surprisingly, they provoke an irritated reaction from the teacher that mirrors her own discomfort about having to do all this boring work all by herself.

Most of the students in Mrs. Perkins's fifth-grade social studies class are busily writing the capitals of the fifty states on their maps. Brandon looks around at his classmates as they work and then flings up his right hand and waves it frantically. Writing the assignment for the day on the chalkboard, Mrs. Perkins does not see his hand. But instead of putting his hand down and working, Brandon keeps on waving his hand and trying to attract her attention. After several minutes, he puts his hand down with a look of frustration. But he does not return to work. He sits passively, watching Mrs. Perkins writing on the chalkboard.

Because the performance-oriented underachiever is constantly worrying about whether her schoolwork is good enough to satisfy her unvalidated parent, she would like to ask the teacher frequently for help, especially on quizzes or tests. But because she fears that her questions, like her work, may not be quite right and will be met with a disappointed or critical response from the teacher, she, too, has trouble asking appropriately for help. Instead, she either sits at her desk, agonizing over her paper and telling herself that she ought to know all the answers, or becomes so disorganized with anxiety when she fails to understand everything perfectly that she cannot use the support the teacher offers.

Mr. Weiss looks up to see Carla standing beside his desk for the third time during the geometry test. "Carla, don't tell me you have another question?" he asks wryly.

"I just don't understand question twelve," Carla moans, an anguished look on her face.

"Now, we've gone over that in class several times," Mr. Weiss replies patiently. "You just think about it a little bit, and I bet you'll get it."

Looking downcast, Carla returns slowly to her seat. She feels the tears welling up in her eyes and fights hard to keep them down. By now she is so anxious that she has forgotten how to do some of the other problems, too.

THE TEACHER'S RESPONSE TO THE UNDERACHIEVER'S BIDS FOR ASSISTANCE

If the insecurely attached child is fortunate enough to have teachers who are sensitive and responsive to his needs in the early grades, his maladaptive internal world can be modified in a more positive direction. The power of teachers to shape the child's images of himself and others is greater in the primary grades than at any other period in his school years because those images are less solidified. To help the insecurely attached child effectively, the teacher must intuitively respond to the child's bid for assistance not only in terms of the *content* of his request but in terms of the *feelings* behind that request. That is, she must not only offer help with a particular task but also convey her warm, enthusiastic support for the child's learning process. Reminding him of the sound that short *e* makes, for example, without also conveying her confidence in his ability to master phonics will leave his ineffective internal beliefs unchanged.

Because of the multiple demands on her time and attention, however, the teacher often delays coming to his aid and sometimes fails to recognize his bid for help altogether. As we have seen, the securely attached child takes the tardiness or failure of the teacher to respond to his request for assistance in stride. He may seek help from a classmate or try again on his own, but he will not experience her temporary lack of responsiveness as overwhelmingly disruptive. He continues to believe in his own competence and in his capacity to receive help. So he persists at his work, and when he finally solves the problem, he takes pride in his success. If he is unable to reach a solution, he goes on to something else in the firm belief that help will ultimately arrive.

But for the insecurely attached child, the teacher's lack of responsiveness evokes his parents' earlier difficulty in responding sensitively to his signals for comfort or assistance. It confirms his unconscious view of others as unhelpful and his view of himself as unworthy of being helped. Depending on his level of stress and his usual method of dealing with frustration, he may cope with this perceived rejection by becoming more demanding, giving up, or getting angry.

Miss O'Brian is working with a reading group in a corner of the room as the other third graders write sentences using the vocabulary words on the chalkboard. Forrest springs abruptly out of his seat and dashes up to her.

"I don't know this word," he says, pointing to one of the words on the chalkboard.

"Forrest, we just went over all those words," replies his teacher in an irritated tone. "See if you can figure it out."

An angry expression on his face, Forrest slowly walks back to his seat, kicking the chairs of several students on his way.

"Miss O'Brian, Forrest's kicking my chair!" complains one of his victims.

Looking up from the reading group, Miss O'Brian warns, "Forrest, keep your feet to yourself!" and adds, "Don't forget now, children, you need to write your sentences twice today."

"I'm going to write 'em once!" Forrest mutters under his breath and slams his pencil down on his desk so hard that he breaks the point.

THE PERPETUATION OF
MALADAPTIVE BELIEFS AT SCHOOL

As the insecurely attached child proceeds through school, a vicious circle is set in motion. Because his maladaptive internal beliefs prevent him from fully investing in his learning experiences, he does not discover that he is, after all, competent to perform his school tasks. Moreover, because he seeks help in inappropriate ways, he does not discover that his teacher is an available and willing source of assistance. As a result, he is unable to modify his rigid, inappropriate views of himself and others in more realistic, positive directions. Instead, filtering his school experiences through the negative perspective of his internal world, he continues to see only his own inadequacy and the teacher's unhelpfulness. As time goes on, his maladaptive attempts to find some measure of security and validation at school provoke his teachers and classmates to treat him in the very ways that his internal images predict—by being critical, unhelpful, and rejecting. With his negative expectations confirmed, his distorted internal world becomes more and more resistant to change.

Part Three

Pathways
to
Achievement

5.

The Problem with the Solution:
Why Treatments Fail

The frustrated parents of an underachiever tend to think of underachievement as a problem with a single cause and a single solution. The problem is the child's poor academic performance. Since the child appears to be of at least average ability, the cause of his underachievement must be his lack of effort. Given this assumption, the solution to the problem is obvious: The child needs to try harder. On the basis of this conception of the problem, the cause, and the solution, parents usually attempt to treat underachievement by increasing their control over the child's behavior. In other words, they try to make the child try harder.

TREATMENT BY MONITORING

To make the underachiever try harder, parents often begin by increasing their monitoring of his academic work. By far the most common of these monitoring attempts is what I call the *assignment book routine*.

THE ASSIGNMENT BOOK ROUTINE

This treatment strategy for underachievement is so widespread that most parents reading this book have probably tried it already, perhaps on several occasions. According to the assignment book routine, the child is supposed to keep a record of his homework assignments in a notebook, usually a small memo pad that can be tucked into a pocket or purse. The assignment book routine has several variations ranging from loose to strict monitoring. In the most common version, the child writes down his assignments for each subject, and the teacher signs or initials each entry to verify that the child's record is accurate. If no assignment is given, the child writes, "No homework." Parental involvement in the assignment book routine also varies from minimal to considerable. Parents may have the child use the assignment book to keep track of his homework on his own, they may require him to show it to them each day, or they may initial entries or write comments daily to indicate to the teacher that they have seen the recorded assignments.

On the face of it, the assignment book routine looks wonderfully simple and effective because it lets parents know what the child has to do so they can make sure he does it. In all my years of working with underachievers, however, I've found that in those rare instances in which the assignment book routine did seem to work, the child's drop in academic performance was related to some minor difficulty or sudden change in circumstances that was quickly resolved. In cases in which the full-blown underachievement pattern has been present, I have never seen this method work when it was the only intervention. A strategy that addresses only the product of underachievement (failure to do homework) and not the process that creates it (maladaptive internal views of the self and others) is incapable of curing it. What usually happens is that the assignment book routine works for two days. After that, the teachers end up having to call the underachiever up to their desks so they can sign the book. Then he stops showing the book to his teachers. Then he loses it. Then the child's teachers get angry that they went to all this trouble to try to help the child, and the parents get angry that the solution they were hoping would work isn't working, and all the adults are angrier and more frustrated than they were in the beginning.

Another problem with the assignment book routine is that teachers and parents have difficulty using it in a positive manner. When this strategy fails to solve the problem in a short period and the same behaviors that have been sabotaging the child's academic performance begin sabotaging this treatment strategy as well, their frustration is bound to increase. Impatient for change, teachers often begin writing what children accurately call "bad notes," and negative comments on the underachiever's performance, behavior, or both begin appearing on the pages of the assignment book:

"I want you to know that Martha didn't finish her classwork today."

"Peter finally turned in his science report, but he still owes me five lab write-ups."

"Alice spent too much time socializing instead of working today."

Upon receiving such a note, parents, believing correctly that the teacher expects them to review such comments with the child, confront him with his failings, which only serves to reinforce his view of others as critical and unhelpful rather than supportive. The parents may even write a note back to the teacher, acknowledging the comments and further confirming the child's negative view of himself:

"We are sorry to hear about Martha's poor showing. We will talk to her about trying harder."

The child perceives that the system that is supposed to be helping him feel more positive about school is being used by his teachers and parents to communicate negative messages about him to each other. Is it any wonder that so many assignment books vanish so rapidly?

When he was asked where his memo book was, third-grade Sammy admitted tearfully, "I threw away my assignment pad because I don't want my teacher to write any more bad notes."

At home, the parents also have trouble keeping the assignment book routine positive. In their anxiety to help the underachiever become more productive, they may focus so much on trying to make the system work that opportunities for constructive communication about school experiences are lost. Daily interrogations about the assignment book replace opportunities for emotional sharing about the child's school experiences:

> *"Paul, why haven't you shown me your assignment book today? Is this it? Look at the shape it's in! Why don't you have anything written down for English? Is this really Mr. Johnson's signature? How can you read this scribbling? And what's this Mrs. Peabody says about your making trouble for the substitute teacher yesterday?"*

As it becomes clear that the assignment book routine has failed to make the child try harder, parents may seek to increase their monitoring, but this time, over the teacher rather than the child. In desperation, they may ask him to call them every day to report on the child's performance and homework or to call if the child fails to hand in an assignment. Even if the teacher initially attempts to meet such demands, he will ultimately refuse to continue when it becomes evident that reporting to the parents has no effect on the child's productivity. When the teacher declines to take over the monitoring function for the parents, they may feel that he is refusing to help the child and turn the full force of their frustration against him, making school an even less secure base for the child. All too often, the end result of the assignment book routine is to make the relationship between home and school more adversarial. Each side feels that it has tried to cooperate in managing the child's work and that other side hasn't kept its part of the bargain. For the underachiever himself, his negative self-image is now doubly reinforced by the failure of efforts by both home and school to provide him with meaningful assistance. He is confirmed in the conviction that he is, in the words of one unhappy seventh grader who had just lost his assignment book for the third time, "a real screw-up."

THE INDIVIDUAL PROGRESS REPORT

Another popular method of trying to treat the underachiever by increasing control over his behavior is the individual progress report. Typically, the progress report consists of a list of classroom behaviors the underachiever has difficulty performing (listening to instructions, turning in classwork, bringing materials to class) that are rated by the teacher on a scale from poor to excellent. An example is provided below.

SAM'S DAILY NOTE

BEHAVIOR	RATING				
	poor				excellent
1. Staying in seat	1	2	3	4	5
2. Beginning assignments on time	1	2	3	4	5
3. Completing assignments	1	2	3	4	5
4. Turning in homework	1	2	3	4	5

_____   _____
Teacher's Signature   *Date*

The progress report may be simply a record of information for the parents about the child's school performance, or it may be linked to rewards provided at home. For elementary school students, progress reports are usually designed to be used daily, whereas for middle and high school students, they are typically used weekly. A variation of the individual progress report is the behavior contract. A behavior contract consists of a written agreement developed by the parents, child, and teacher that states the type and quality of performance that the child will accomplish and is signed by all parties to underscore its importance. Rewards or privileges at home are linked to satisfactory performance.

Individual progress reports are currently very popular with parents and professionals alike as a treatment for underachievement and a host of other school problems. On the face of it, they appear to be a straightforward and effective method of charting the child's classroom behavior and performance. If they are linked to home-based rewards, they also appear to offer the underachiever motivation for improvement. Unfortunately, progress reports are neither as simple to use nor as motivating as they appear. For one thing, developing and maintaining an effective monitoring system requires considerable effort on the part of parents, teachers, and students. A progress report (with or without rewards) must be developed, forms must be given regularly to the teacher, the teacher must take class time daily or weekly to complete the form, the child must collect the report from the teacher and bring it home, and the parents must review the child's progress with her and provide the agreed-upon rewards, if those are part of the system. Just as with the assignment book routine, the risks are tremendous that the parents will become overly intrusive, the teacher will write negative comments, and the underachiever will sabotage the entire process.

The major problem with progress reports and behavior contracts, however, is that adults confuse the ability of these methods to *monitor* behavior with their ability to *modify* behavior. Simply charting what is happening is not enough to change behavior. Instead of creating positive change, all too often progress reports simply chronicle the child's continuing failure.

Tony's parents were frantic to try to help their very bright but very inattentive and unproductive second-grade son overcome his problems. In an effort to provide regular feedback for them on Tony's classroom performance, the school psychologist developed a daily progress report. At the end of each day, the teacher was to rate two of Tony's behaviors as follows:

	Yes	No
Tony paid attention in class.	1	0
Tony did his work in class.	1	0

The psychologist told the parents that monitoring only two behaviors would help Tony focus and would increase his motivation to improve. Moreover, in an effort to lower the standard of performance, he selected only two rating categories. The first day, Tony took home two zeros. The second day he took home another two zeros. For the four

weeks that the progress report was in effect, Tony earned nearly all ze-
ros, and his behavior and productivity actually deteriorated. Tony, his
teacher, and his parents were devastated.

The psychologist had tried to insure success by limiting the behaviors
to be monitored and including only two rating categories. But by select-
ing the very behaviors in which underachievers are least competent and
using so few ratings that small increments of change could not be ob-
served, he created a system that was doomed to failure. Moreover, the
use of a zero rating reinforced Tony's feelings of inadequacy. Now he
wasn't just a poor student. He was a zero.

When adults attempt to treat underachievement by increasing their
control over the child, the underachiever may temporarily welcome
these efforts to manage her work for her because it helps her avoid the
conflicting feelings aroused by independent functioning. But telling
her that she has to learn to accept responsibility for her work and then
giving her less rather than more control over it reduces rather than en-
hances her self-efficacy. When a treatment based on control is ended,
any improvement in achievement is likely to end as well.

TREATMENT BY CHANGE OF PLACEMENT

RETENTION

Although retention has long been used as a treatment for poor school
performance, the question of retention for underachievers revolves
around whether their failure to attain grade-level objectives derives
from lack of academic skills or lack of effort. Because teachers and parents of underachievers believe that they are capable of doing the work,
underachievers are often promoted or "placed" in the next grade despite their poor showing. ("Placed" is a term indicating that the student
did not meet all of the requirements for promotion but was moved to
the next grade anyway.) Underachievers are also often promoted because their teachers are so sick and tired of trying to motivate them
that, consciously or unconsciously, they want them out of that grade so
they will no longer have to deal with them. It is not uncommon for un-

derachievers to be "placed" two, three, or even more times during elementary and middle school. These unearned placements are highly detrimental to the underachiever's academic skills and his internal perspective, however. Although the underachiever's typically good oral language skills may fool teachers and parents into believing that his other skills are equally well developed, it is much more likely that years of inattention and poor study habits have eroded many competencies, leaving him with a diminished base of knowledge compared with his peers. Moreover, being promoted for hypothesized ability rather than actual productivity reinforces his sense of entitlement and belief that school norms apply to others, not to him.

"I got 3 Fs and I passed to fifth grade anyway!" Laura was overheard boasting to a friend. "I told you they wouldn't keep me in fourth grade!" She tossed her head defiantly.

Not all underachievers escape the consequences of their lack of productivity. At some point in the middle or high school years, their cumulative skill deficiencies catch up with them. Unable to achieve even the minimum standards for promotion, they are finally retained or forced to repeat a subject in order to move on to the next grade. In fact, whereas in the near past, having a child repeat a grade was considered a disgrace, today's parents often seek to have an underachiever retained, especially if he is in kindergarten or first grade. Even though large-scale studies and clinical experience alike indicate that retention does not benefit children in terms of academic achievement or social adjustment, many parents and teachers continue to believe that retention will help the underachiever "grow up and catch up." In elementary and middle school, parents have considerable input into promotion or placement decisions, and their requests are usually honored. At the high school level, however, where promotion and graduation are linked to earned academic credits, parents have little or no influence on the decision. Retention is by subject rather than grade, with the total number of passed academic credits determining in which grade a student belongs.

Although retention forces the underachiever to suffer the consequences of his behavior, parents should bear in mind that retaining the underachiever is no guarantee that better grades will result if it is the only intervention. The ineffective internal belief system that gives rise to underachievement is still very much present, whether the child repeats a grade or is promoted to the next. Rather than motivating the underachiever to perform, retention is likely to solidify his image of himself as bad and stupid and his image of others as unresponsive to his needs. At the end of another year, his parents and teachers will probably be facing the same dilemma.

ACCELERATION

"Alphonso is really a very smart boy, you know," his mother explained to his third-grade teacher. "I think he gets into trouble and doesn't do his work because he's bored in your class. I'm going to ask the principal to move him to fourth grade where he'll be more challenged."

Parents of an underachiever may wonder whether their child is simply bored with regular instruction and would do better if she were promoted to the next higher grade where she would be "challenged." They are especially likely to wonder about academic acceleration if she is also inattentive and disruptive in class. In the not too distant past, acceleration or skipping a grade was a frequent remedy for the bright but bored child and was made on the basis of teacher and parent recommendation without formal testing. In most school districts today, grade acceleration is an infrequent, formalized procedure requiring a battery of ability and achievement tests administered by the school psychologist and an array of teacher ratings on social and academic behaviors. Exceptionally capable children are usually accelerated *within* a grade by means of flexible scheduling that permits them to switch classes for those subjects in which they far excel their peers. The child may, for example, take third-grade math but go to a fifth-grade classroom for reading. This practice has long been used at the high school level, enabling students to take courses offered by local colleges, but it is now being implemented in elementary and middle schools as well.

Given the underachiever's constant complaints that school is "boring" and that she "knows all that stuff anyway," it is understandable that parents might believe acceleration would help motivate her to work harder. As we have seen, it can be very difficult to distinguish between a gifted student who is genuinely bored with the pace of the regular curriculum and an underachiever who uses the term *bored* to describe her inner state of anxiety and emptiness. In a few cases, grade acceleration may be appropriate for the child who is achieving at a truly superior level *at the present time*. It is not appropriate as an effort to make the underachiever try harder or behave better.

Despite the great concern that parents tend to focus on the child's grade placement, whether the child is retained or accelerated is not, ultimately, the most important issue. Her attitudes toward herself and toward learning, not her grade placement, are what determine the degree to which she is motivated to succeed in school.

TREATMENT BY REWARD

One afternoon I received a call from the father of a seventh grader who was certain that he had at last found the solution to his son's poor academic performance. "We told Ronald that we'll give him fifty dollars if he makes all As on his report card," he told me excitedly. "That ought to do it!"

Unfortunately for Ronald and his parents, even a large cash reward was not enough to help him try harder. His next report card showed the same Ds and Fs as had the previous ones, leaving his parents more frustrated than ever.

Another common treatment parents use to try to make the underachiever try harder is to offer her some kind of reward for improved academic performance. Parents of longtime underachievers are especially likely to promise cash or expensive gifts for better grades. Parents of chronic underachievers are also likely to link large rewards to unrealistic improvements in performance, such as straight As for a child who has been making Ds and Fs for the last two years. Just as the underachiever selects unrealistically high goals to compensate for her sense of inferiority, so her parents may set exalted goals for improvement in the unconscious wish to undo the underachiever's past poor record—and their own frustrated wishes for the child. Such goal selection by parents is not only unrealistic, given the multiplicity of ineffective habits that must be modified for such a drastic change in academic performance, but it also reinforces the underachiever's belief that only superior performance can make up for her fundamental inadequacy.

WHAT'S WRONG WITH REWARDS?

Too much time between the behavior and the reward. One of the problems with giving rewards for good grades is that the reward is delivered too long after the behaviors that lead to those good grades (bringing the appropriate materials to class, paying attention, completing classwork and homework, studying for tests, and so forth) to serve as an effective reinforcer. As much as the child may want the reward, he simply cannot sustain the effort necessary over the six- or nine-week grading period to earn it. After all, persistence is one of his major problems!

In an attempt to provide reinforcement throughout the long grading period, parents, following the advice of some parenting books, may implement elaborate behavior management systems, with completion of homework, daily grades, or other interim measures related to accumulating points, which can then be cashed in for rewards. Although giving frequent rewards seems as if it would be more effective than promising a single large reward at the end of the report card period, the increase in parental monitoring necessary to maintain such a system actually discourages independent effort, and the risk of perpetuating an overly intrusive management style outweighs any possible benefits.

Negative messages about the true source of motivation. Another problem with giving material rewards for academic achievement is the message this strategy gives to the child: External motivation can substitute for internal motivation. On the contrary, research and my own work with underachievers and their families demonstrate that giving rewards can have an effect on motivation opposite to the one desired. That is, rewards *decrease* the intrinsic value of the rewarded activity. Rewards tell the child that learning is not rewarding enough to be engaged in for its own sake; to be rewarding, it must be accompanied by material gains. Promising the child a gift if his performance improves teaches him to work for the reward and not for the thrill of increasing his competence, the intrinsic interest of the activity, or a desire to please his parents. Although parents mean to encourage motivation when they promise to supply external reinforcement such as money or toys for better grades, the message is: "Your schoolwork isn't interesting enough to be rewarding in and of itself. We, your parents, know this, so we must give you an external reason to do it."

Who gets rewarded? When parents consider using rewards to motivate the underachiever, a problem arises if other children in the family are performing satisfactorily. In such cases, who gets rewarded? Although parents may believe that rewards are not necessary for the achievers, offering material incentives for good academic performance only to the underachiever may have negative effects on the achievement and attitudes of siblings who have no opportunity to earn them.

On the advice of a psychologist, the parents of an underachieving eighth grader set up a program of rewards by which he could earn points toward a stereo system of his own, something he very much desired. His tenth-grade brother, who was achieving satisfactorily in school, bitterly resented that his good performance was unrewarded, while, from his point of view, his brother was being rewarded for being bad. After a few months, the parents reluctantly placed the older son on a similar reward system, but the damage had already been done. The older son felt as if his previous hard work had gone unnoticed and his grades and attitude toward school declined, even though he, too, could now earn rewards. Moreover, after the eighth grader had earned enough points to purchase an expensive stereo system, his parents had to devise additional rewards to keep him working. When he demanded a motorcycle, the parents sought another therapist.

Rewards lose their value over time. Another problem associated with giving rewards for improvement in grades is that over time, the perceived value of rewards tends to diminish, whether they are special snacks, television time, toys, or even money. Although this satiation ef-

fect occurs for all rewards, it is especially likely to occur when the behavior that must be performed is stressful or tedious, such as studying,
paying attention in class, or completing assignments. Parents who set
up reward systems soon find that they have difficulty continually devis-
ing rewards that satisfy the child enough to make him do his work and
that do not exhaust or bankrupt them. Parents can go on just so many
trips to amusement parks, sit through just so many movies, make just so
many special snacks, and purchase just so many gifts. Over time, parents who rely on rewards to motivate schoolwork find that the child
asks for larger and larger rewards for appropriate behavior.

> *Fifth-grade Angelo was now reluctantly doing his homework to earn
> time playing video games, but his homework seldom found its way to
> the teacher's desk. In frustration, his father brought him to my office for
> a conference.*
>
> *"What would it take for you to want to turn your homework in?" I
> asked Angelo.*
>
> *His eyes lit up immediately. "Cable TV!" he cried triumphantly,
> glancing at his father, who threw up his hands in exasperation.*

Ending rewards. In fact, one of the greatest problems associated with
giving tangible rewards is that eventually the child must be weaned
from them. Although authors recommending home-based reinforcement systems claim that the child can gradually be weaned to social rewards, such as praise, or self-rewards, that is, praising oneself, it is by no
means clear whether the shift from external to internal reinforcement
really occurs in home-based reinforcement programs, because most
studies claiming that rewards are effective do not indicate whether
gains were maintained after the rewards were withdrawn. Instead, the
withdrawal of rewards is likely to lead to a decrease in the frequency of
the previously rewarded behaviors and an increase in the child's resentment at his inability to earn additional rewards.

Reinforcement of ineffective modes of thinking. By far the most negative
consequence of using rewards, however, is the effect on the underachiever's internal view of himself and others. The child who is offered
external incentives for good school performance reasons, "Why do my

parents need to reward or bribe me to perform? It must be because I am incapable of performing satisfactorily without rewards." Thus rewards for achievement actually strengthen the child's image of himself as inferior and incompetent. Similarly, rewards, especially large rewards, reinforce his belief that his parents value the external product of his performance (grades) more than his internal growth (feelings of competence).

Offering rewards as a treatment for underachievement never leads to increased motivation and very seldom leads to better grades. At the most, it causes the child to engage in frenzied efforts to improve for a few days or weeks. After a short time, however, the tedium of completing daily work and studying sets in, and the underachiever's burst of enthusiasm rapidly diminishes. If the goal of treatment is to develop a self-directed learner, tangible rewards ultimately create attitudes that interfere with that goal.

TREATMENT BY PUNISHMENT

When treatment by monitoring and treatment by rewards fail to produce results, parents are likely to resort in desperation to punishment.

"Billy, there'll be no more TV until those grades come up."

"Sandy, if you think you're going to talk on the phone to your friends on school nights after that terrible report card, you have another think coming."

"A D in Spanish? That's it, Tina, you can forget driving the car for the rest of the six weeks!"

Once parents start using punishment, they are likely to have trouble giving it up because of its reinforcing properties. Punishment is reinforcing to the parents of the underachiever for several reasons. First, administering some form of punishment makes parents feel temporarily more in control of a situation that makes them feel helpless. Second, on a short-term basis, the use of punishment may increase the child's compliance with parental injunctions to stay in her room during study time, do her homework, and so on, especially when the child believes that compliance will result in the speedy restoration of privileges.

Punishment is also reinforcing for the underachiever, but not in the manner that her parents intend. Although punishment is ineffective in making her try harder, it is highly effective in solidifying her view of herself as unlovable and her view of others as unhelpful. If treatment by punishment continues, it is likely to motivate her to act out her image of herself as bad and dumb by misbehaving in school or at home or by performing even more poorly academically.

As it becomes clear that the present level of punishment has been unsuccessful in forcing the underachiever to improve, parents tend to increase it in their desperate efforts to find some treatment that works. As the cycle of parental punishment, followed by negative reaction by the child, followed by more punitive measures continues, one day of restriction can rapidly escalate to six weeks. Because families who punish are often families in which the child has an overly involved relationship with one parent while the other parent is emotionally distant, these escalated punishments are seldom carried out. Instead, they are rescinded by the overly involved parent, who, fearful of losing the child's affection, eventually forces the distant parent to capitulate.

> "I think Jimmy's father comes down too hard on him about his schoolwork," confided Mrs. Pearce. "He yells and slams doors and says he's on restriction for two weeks and then Jimmy yells back and stomps up to his room and I end up mediating between the two of them. But after a while I can usually get his father to see things my way."

Corporal Punishment

Sometimes parents become so frustrated with what seems to be the child's stubborn refusal to do her work despite her ability to do it that they resort to physical punishment. Such punishment may be delivered as part of a previously issued ultimatum ("If I hear from your teacher one more time that you didn't hand in your homework, I'm going to spank you"). On other occasions, arguments over grades and homework deteriorate to the point that the parent spanks or slaps the child out of sheer frustration.

The problem with corporal punishment is that there is no logical connection between a swat on the behind and low grades or classroom misbehavior. Physical punishment only endows schoolwork—and the parents—with even more negative associations than before and confirms the child's image of herself as bad and unlovable. After all, if she were good, her parents wouldn't cause her pain and embarrassment. She will continue to act badly in accordance with that self-image and may even come to believe, as her parents seem to believe, that only punishment can drive out her badness.

> *Bobby, a slightly built kindergartner with a sad expression, talked openly about his poor grades and his deplorable classroom behavior. "I just don't do my work and I get in trouble all the time," he admitted plaintively.*
>
> *"What do you think would help you do your work better?" I asked him.*
>
> *He looked at me out of his bright blue eyes and answered without hesitation: "A bigger belt."*

The Ultimatum

"If you don't pull up your grades, you're off the swim team!"

"If you don't pass math, you can't go out during the week all second semester!"

Parents often issue punishments in the form of ultimatums. Ultimatums resemble rewards in that they take effect some time in the future and are contingent upon performance. But just as long-term rewards are too distant in time from the relevant behavior to promote greater persistence, so ultimatums are ineffective in changing children's behavior. On the contrary, instead of encouraging the child to try harder, an ultimatum only increases his anxiety so that he is even less capable of investing in his schoolwork. As the date of the administration of the threatened consequences approaches, the child becomes more and more inattentive and disruptive in class in anticipation that a treasured privilege will be taken away or a punishment inflicted. Sooner or later, the futility of punishment in improving achievement becomes all too evident to parents who use it.

> *"I've taken away Mark's radio and stereo. I've grounded him for six weeks. We've taken away everything we can possibly take away and he's still not handing in his work," said the distressed father of a ninth grader. "He's too old to spank, but I don't know what else to do!"*

As with escalating punishments, parents are often unable to bring themselves to act on the ultimatum when the time arrives and the child's academic performance has not reached the required standard. Or one parent is willing to act on the threat, but the other prevents its execution. In the end, both the parents and the child know that the parents cannot *force* the child to achieve. As one eleventh grader told me with a defiant gleam in his eyes, "Maybe my parents can take away my guitar, but they can't take away my bad grades."

BOARDING SCHOOL: THE ULTIMATE ULTIMATUM

In an effort to convince the child of their determination that he must improve his schoolwork, some parents may threaten to send him away from home to a private day school, boarding school, or military academy if he does not try harder. Frustrated at the child's continuing underachievement and the failure of their own efforts to help him, the parents issue the ultimate ultimatum:

> *"If you don't stop goofing off and start doing your work, we're going to send you to military school. They'll make you do your work there!"*

Parents' use of a change of school as a threat is very different from the genuine consideration of educational options other than his present placement. Although they may consciously see a day or boarding

school as a place where the child can receive more individual attention, they may unconsciously view it as a place where the child "won't
be able to get away with anything," especially in the case of a military
boarding school. They may believe that such a school will finally be
able to do what they have been unable to do: "make" the child achieve.
Most parents who deliver such an ultimatum have no real intention of
carrying it out. They issue it in the hope that it will convince the child
that they are serious about his need to improve and out of the conviction that the child's thoughts and actions are under his conscious control. Rather than making him work harder, however, such a threat
further undermines his tenuous sense of security by confirming his belief that he is so unlovable even his own parents don't want him
around. The voices in his inner world telling him he is worthless have
been right all along. Nevertheless, the immediate effect of a threat to
send the child away to school may be a temporary spurt of effort as the
child tries desperately to improve. But invariably his performance dete-
riorates because he is even more anxious and less able to concentrate
on his lessons. Moreover, using boarding school as an ultimatum makes
the underachiever even more reluctant to seek help from his parents.
On the contrary, he will redouble his efforts to conceal his academic
problems from them. Or he may become even more provocative, disruptive, and unproductive in an unconscious attempt to put an end to
his terrible tension and provoke his parents into carrying out what he
believes is an inevitable rejection on their part. Fear is a poor motivator
of achievement in the short term and even poorer in the long term.

A NEW SOLUTION TO AN OLD PROBLEM

At this point, parents may be asking, If monitoring doesn't work and
rewards and punishments don't work, what are we supposed to do—
nothing? The frustrated and discouraged parents of an underachiever
are often so caught up in trying to make the child work that they can
see only two treatment alternatives: increasing their control over him
or giving up altogether. But there is another choice besides these two
extremes. Instead of trying to change the child, parents must do some-

thing much more difficult. *They must change themselves*. That is, parents must change the ways in which they interact and communicate with the underachiever. It is these changes that will enable him to alter his distorted views of himself and the others in his environment and at last change the maladaptive behaviors that derive from those faulty perceptions.

6.

Opening the Door to Change:

Constructive Communication Strategies

To help the underachiever become a happy and successful learner, his parents must help him modify the maladaptive internal world that lies behind the mystery of his underachievement. Just as the parents, in their early interactions with the child, unwittingly contributed to the development of views of the self and others that have interfered with achievement, so changing the nature of those interactions now can shape those views in ways that support high achievement. The remainder of Part Three presents a comprehensive treatment program by which parents can help the child develop the positive beliefs about his own competency and the ability of others to help him that lead to school success. This chapter first describes how parents can open communication with the underachiever by learning to translate his mystifying and frustrating language and then outlines five constructive communication strategies, which form the heart of the treatment program. Both Chapter 6 and Chapter 7 present strategies by which parents can help the underachiever become more competent at home and at school.

CONSTRUCTIVE AND
DESTRUCTIVE COMMUNICATION

"Every afternoon it's the same old thing," fumed fourteen-year-old Janice. *"The minute I step in the door, my mother says, 'How was school today? Do you have any homework?' It drives me crazy!"*

"I know Janice doesn't like it when I ask her about school," her mother acknowledged. "But I'm so worried about her grades that I just can't help it. I'm afraid if I don't try to talk to her about school, she'll do even worse!"

Contrary to what appears on the surface, underachievers *do* want to communicate with their parents. Because of their distorted views of themselves and others, however, they have trouble expressing their need for love and support effectively. Trying to communicate with underachievers is like trying to walk through a mine field—one false step can produce an explosion! Nevertheless, even underachievers with a defiant "I don't care" attitude are yearning, deep down, for a chance to share their painful feelings with their parents.

Steve's parents had made many attempts to talk to their sullen and withdrawn tenth-grade son about his poor grades. Despite excellent test scores, he was failing two classes and making Cs in his other subjects. Hoping that he would feel freer to talk about his academic performance with someone outside the family, Steve's parents asked me to meet with him. At one point, I asked him what he would wish for if he could have one wish. The lanky six-footer brushed his long hair out of his eyes and answered without hesitation, "I wish my dad and I could talk better."

HOW TO SPEAK MARTIAN: LEARNING THE LANGUAGE OF THE UNDERACHIEVER

Because communication is a two-way process, the first step in communicating constructively with the underachiever is learning to understand the language he uses. I like to refer to this language as *Martian* because it seems so alien to parents that they often feel as if they are trying to communicate with an extraterrestrial being. Indeed, the underachiever unconsciously uses language not to communicate his true feelings but to disguise them. Because he anticipates unhelpful or rejecting responses from others, communicating his secret fears about his own inadequacy would be too dangerous to risk. As a result, his language is designed to protect his fragile self-esteem by preventing—not facilitating—access to his thoughts and feelings.

Although the underachiever has great difficulty in expressing his distress directly, paradoxically he is a master at communicating to others *how* he feels. He unconsciously uses language in such a way as to induce the person trying to communicate with him to feel the way he does. Consequently, the parent who responds to the surface content rather than the underlying meaning of the underachiever's communications soon finds himself feeling as anxious, angry, and helpless as the underachiever. Under these circumstances, communication rapidly becomes destructive rather than constructive, with accusations or gloomy predictions by the parent, followed by angry outbursts or withdrawal by the child. Deciphering the real message of the underachiever's communications so that the task of modifying his faulty internal beliefs can begin takes practice and patience.

The Use of Absolutes

In the underachiever's language, things are all or nothing, never in between. His sentences resound with such words as *nobody, all, totally, always,* and *never.*

> "*I'm* never *going to be able to understand* all *of these geometry theorems.*"

> "*The* whole *class is going to fail French because* no one *has* any *idea of what's going on.*"

In part, the underachiever's use of absolutes reflects his perfectionistic goals. Because, deep down, he believes that he is incompetent, only perfection (all goodness) can compensate for his inadequacy (all badness). His use of absolutes is also an unconscious attempt to induce others to understand his painful feelings, which he experiences as truly extreme. His words eloquently convey his conviction that *everything* is awful and things will *never* get better. Unfortunately, however, as adults listen to his chronicle of absolutes, which seem to preclude the possibility that he can either help himself or accept help from others, they find themselves feeling so hopeless that they react defensively—and unhelpfully. They may try to argue him out of making such extreme pronouncements.

"Don't say you'll never understand geometry. You'll catch on in time."

"Somebody in your French class must be doing well. Everybody can't be flunking."

Or they may tell the child how to behave so that the extreme situations he describes will not occur.

"You'd understand geometry if you didn't put off studying for your tests until the last minute."

"If you paid more attention in French class, you wouldn't be flunking."

Eventually, parents may get so frustrated that they end up using absolutes themselves:

"You'll never get into a decent college if you don't buckle down and study."

"Nobody has to put up with the kind of aggravation with their kids that I do."

Efforts to make the underachiever relinquish his use of absolutes by arguing with him or telling him what to do differently are doomed to failure. These responses only serve to reinforce his conviction that others cannot help him with his plight. Instead of arguing with the underachiever or giving him advice, parents can open the door to constructive communication by empathizing with the painful feelings that lie behind the absolutes:

CHILD: *I'll never get a good grade from Mr. Beechum.*
PARENT: *It seems really difficult to do well in Mr. Beechum's geome-
         try class.*
CHILD: *Yeah. He gives tons of work and he never explains any-
         thing so anybody can understand it.*
PARENT: *It sounds like there's a lot of work and it can be pretty con-
         fusing.*
CHILD: *Confusing is right! (Pause) Do you think you could help me
         with this homework set of problems?*

DISAVOWING RESPONSIBILITY AND
DISPLACING WORRY

Many of the underachiever's communications disavow responsibility
for her own behavior. Whatever has happened, it isn't because of something she did (or didn't do). The problem lies somewhere in the external world: too much work, boring assignments, noisy classmates, or
mean teachers.

   *"What's the use of social studies? It's boring and has nothing to do with
   my life!"*

   *"I can't pay attention in Spanish because the other kids are clowning
   around all the time."*

The underachiever assigns responsibility to external factors because
she believes that she is powerless to control her own behavior. And if
she is powerless, what happens to her cannot possibly be the result of
her own actions. When her parents try to defend the situation or person she is blaming for her problems ("Social studies is useful for everybody"; "The Spanish teacher says the other students aren't bothering
you"), she will not be convinced they are correct. She will only be more
convinced than ever that no one, not even her own parents, understands her feelings.
   Despite her failure to take responsibility for her own behavior, the

underachiever does communicate her worries to others. She does so, however, *in displaced form*, that is, by talking about other people who are acting in the same ineffective ways that she is. When, for example, the underachiever brings home tales of her classmates' lackluster performance, parents should pay close attention. The statement that "Jeffrey is going to flunk history" signals something about the child's own fear of failure.

If parents respond by rejecting the displacement ("Why don't you worry about your own grades instead of Jeffrey's?"), even this indirect communication will cease. Instead, parents should enter into the displacement and thus provide an opportunity for the child to talk about her own problems.

CHILD: *Jeffrey is going to flunk history.*
PARENT: *Sounds like history isn't going so great for your friend.*
CHILD: *Yeah. He may have to go to summer school. Nobody wants to go to summer school.*
PARENT: *Summer school doesn't sound like much fun. I wonder if any other kids are having the same problem.*
CHILD: *Yeah. Mr. Franks is so tough. (Pause) I think I might be getting an interim in there.*
PARENT: *You might be getting an interim in history?*
CHILD: *Yeah. I didn't do so hot on the last two tests.*
PARENT: *History has really been tough for you lately.*
CHILD: *I guess so. I don't want to have to go to summer school.*
PARENT: *Maybe we could think of some ways you can avoid having that happen.*
CHILD: *Sounds good to me.*

THE AFFIRMATION OF HELPLESSNESS

The underachiever's language characterizes herself as utterly unable to control the events in her life, including her own behavior. Her conversation rings with protestations that whatever she does doesn't make any difference.

"It doesn't matter if I study for my math test. Last time I studied and I still flunked."

"I give up. I'll never understand participles."

Parents find it very difficult to respond constructively to the underachiever's affirmation of helplessness. Their child is telling them that her efforts don't matter and that, by implication, their efforts don't matter either. Feeling ineffective and angry, they are likely to respond unhelpfully, just as the child's internal models lead her to expect. Even if parents attempt to encourage the underachiever ("Of course you can do it!"), her distorted perspective causes her to hear only that she has disappointed them by her failure to "do it" before now.

When the underachiever affirms her own helplessness, parents should focus on communicating their steadfast belief in the child's ability to solve her problems. This is harder than it sounds! It takes practice not to react to her expressions of helplessness by telling her she can do it or offering unwanted advice. Instead, parents should begin by acknowledging the feelings the child is expressing:

"You're really worried about passing math."

"English grammar seems very complicated."

But more is needed here. Parents must make it clear to the child that they are confident she can solve the problem and that they will work with her to find a solution if (and only if) she wants their help.

"It sounds tough, but I'm betting you can find some ways of getting math back on track. If you'd like to talk to me about some of your ideas, I'd be happy to listen and help if I can."

"Getting the hang of English grammar really takes some doing. You know, I bet that anyone who could figure out how to program the VCR as fast as you did can figure out participles. Let me know if you'd like me to look over your homework when you get done."

DEVALUATION: DOWN WITH EVERYTHING AND EVERYBODY

Because the underachiever feels so bad about himself, he projects his negative feelings onto those around him and onto virtually every aspect of his school experience. By devaluing his teachers, subjects, and the entire learning process, he unconsciously tries to defend himself against his own feelings of inferiority. If school is worthless, then his poor performance doesn't matter. The underachiever uses several characteristic phrases in this devaluation process.

Boring

"Mr. Gillam's class is boring."

"Why do we have to do all this boring homework?"

Boring is without a doubt the word underachievers use most frequently to describe their school experiences and to explain their lack of academic success. Although children are sometimes genuinely bored with the unstimulating activities that form part of every school day, *boring* for underachievers reflects not so much their experiences in the school environment as the emptiness of their internal world. The underachiever's use of the word *boring* also reflects his belief that his performance depends not on his internal characteristics, such as his attentiveness and persistence, but on external events. It is the fault of his teachers and the curriculum that he is bored, after all. *Boring* thus explains not only why his performance is poor but also why it does not improve.

Dumb

"That dumb science teacher gives us too much work."

"Why should we have to write a report about some dumb old presidents?"

The underachiever uses the word *dumb* to devalue something he doesn't want to do (classwork, homework, chores, and so forth) or to devalue someone who is trying to make him do it. Someone who is doing better than he is and so triggers his feelings of inadequacy may also earn the label *dumb,* as in, "That dumb old Tyrone thinks he's so smart." Or it may be used to describe goals to which the underachiever secretly aspires but feels incapable of attaining: "Who wants to be in that dumb old gifted class anyway?"

The underachiever's constant use of *dumb* and related terms like *stupid* and *dopey* is guaranteed to alienate the adults who are trying to help him. By association, the parents and teachers urging him to perform the schoolwork he devalues are also "dumb." To understand the true nature of this communication, it is necessary to invert it. In the underachiever's unconscious, *dumb* refers to his view of himself as incompetent. Moreover, *dumb* signifies a permanent condition, one that is not subject to change. Once someone or something is dumb, it will not become smart in the future. Any success he experiences is attributable to luck (*dumb* luck) or some other force outside himself.

I Don't Care

"I don't care if I get a C in reading."

"I don't care if I don't get into college. Who wants to go to school for another four years?"

As the underachiever continues to perform poorly in school, his repertoire of devaluing statements expands to include the ultimate devaluation: *I don't care,* usually delivered in response to his parents' urging him to try harder. *I don't care* really means "I'm feeling so bad about myself and my own ability that it's safer not to care." As years of ineffective work habits take their toll on his academic skills, the underachiever becomes increasingly aware of the widening gap between his perfectionistic goals and his present capacities. Rather than risk humiliation, he tries to disguise his deficiencies by putting forth even less effort and adopting an "I don't care" attitude.

Darryl spent the first part of our counseling session cracking jokes and telling me that he wasn't the least bit worried about his poor grades. He was just a regular, good-time fifteen-year-old whose parents were on his back about his grades. After about twenty minutes, he broke down and, with tears in his eyes, confided that he was going to fail ninth-grade English for the second time.

"I just never figured out present and past tenses and the rest of that grammar," he mumbled in an embarrassed voice. "Up here, they act like you're supposed to know all that stuff already." He paused and added in a sorrowful tone, "If I flunk English again, I'll have to repeat ninth grade or pass it in summer school. How can I pass English in summer school if I can't pass it during the regular year?" He put his head down on the table dejectedly.

STRATEGIES FOR COMMUNICATING CONSTRUCTIVELY WITH THE UNDERACHIEVER

As we have seen, the underachiever's maladaptive internal belief system often leads her to provoke those trying to help her to respond with destructive rather than constructive communication. *Destructive communication* refers to communication that builds internal images of the self as incompetent and internal images of others as unhelpful. In contrast, *constructive communication* helps to create an image of the self that is valuable and competent and images of others who are accessible and responsive. By using constructive communication strategies, parents can help the underachiever express the painful feelings that have been limiting her ability to persist and begin building the kinds of internal supports that lead to academic excellence.

CONSTRUCTIVE COMMUNICATION STRATEGY 1: ALLOWING VERSUS DISAVOWING FEELINGS

CHILD: I hate Mrs. Smith.
PARENT: You don't really hate Mrs. Smith.
CHILD: Yes, I do!

PARENT: *How can you hate someone who's trying so hard to help you? You should be grateful.*

Disavowing feelings is a form of destructive communication in which the child expresses a feeling and the parent invalidates it. As the example above illustrates, disavowing feelings is a two-step process: (1) denying the child's feelings and (2) trying to make him feel differently. Instead of trying to understand the child's emotions, the parent first tells her that she doesn't really feel that way. He then proceeds to tell her how she *should* be feeling.

Why is it so hard for parents to acknowledge that the child sometimes feels bad about her educational experiences? In part, parents discourage the child's expression of negative feelings because they believe that expressing those feelings won't help solve her problems. But parents also discourage the child's expression of painful emotions to avoid reawakening their own negative feelings about school. Some of the negative feelings that the underachiever expresses are about herself, especially about her own competence. The expression of these negative emotions is particularly painful for parents to hear, and thus they are especially quick to disavow them.

CHILD: *I'm just dumb in science, I guess.*
PARENT: *Don't talk like that! You're not dumb and I don't want to hear you saying you are!*

CHILD: *I can't think of stuff to write for my English composition. I guess I'm not very creative.*
PARENT: *That's ridiculous. You're very creative. You just need to sit down and do your work.*

In this example, the parent's need to end the child's distress and his own is so great that he cannot permit her to express and work through her negative emotions. The message the parent intends to convey—his belief in the child's ability—is invalidated by the way he delivers it.

Instead, by using the constructive communication strategy of *allowing feelings*, parents can help the child resolve the painful emotions that are perpetuating her maladaptive views of herself and others and constricting her achievement. The first step in allowing feelings is to *identify* them. It is very important that parents use a warm, nonanxious tone to identify feelings. The child hears very different messages when her parents label her emotions using a critical or anxious tone than when they speak calmly and empathically. Moreover, parents should identify her feelings tentatively so that it does not seem as if they are *telling* the child how she feels.

"You sound kind of upset *about what happened in science class."*

"It seems like you're confused *about what to write for your English assignment."*

Identifying feelings validates the child's inner life in a highly meaningful way. Even if parents' hypotheses fall short of the mark and label her feelings incorrectly, the underachiever will recognize that her parents are making a genuine effort to understand her point of view and will let them know when they have not identified her feelings accurately.

CHILD: *I want to get out of Mrs. Bryant's class. She's going to make me fail for sure. I got a seventy-five on my English composition and she took off five more points for messy handwriting! A bozo could read it!*

PARENT: *It sounds as if you're* disappointed *that Mrs. Bryant took off five points for handwriting.*

CHILD: *I was* mad!

Allowing emotions does *not* mean that parents condone the emotions that are being expressed. What parents support is the child's freedom to express and explore those feelings in a safe environment.

CHILD: *I hate Mrs. Bryant!*

PARENT: *You sound like you're really angry at Mrs. Bryant.*

CHILD: *Yeah! She doesn't grade fair!*

PARENT: *You feel like you don't get a fair deal in her class.*

Nor is allowing feelings the same as giving permission to act out those feelings. The child can be angry at Mrs. Bryant without acting out that anger by misbehaving or by refusing to work in her class. On the contrary, having the freedom to express her feelings at home reduces the possibility that she will act them out at school. When a child knows that she can tell her parents when she feels *bad*, she becomes freer to explore and learn. The child who encounters problems at school but is not allowed to discuss her painful feelings about those problems learns that her base is secure only when her studies are going well, the time when she needs reassurance the least. Moreover, allowing the child to express her feelings makes it much more likely that she will accept her parents' limits on what she actually *does* with those feelings.

CHILD: *I'm so mad I feel like never doing anything for Mrs. Bryant again.*

PARENT: *Sometimes you feel so angry at Mrs. Bryant that you'd like to pay her back by not doing your work, but it's important to stick to your goal of getting good grades in that class.*

CHILD: *Yeah, I guess so. I'll show her. I'll have the best handwriting in class next time!*

CONSTRUCTIVE COMMUNICATION STRATEGY 2: MANAGING EMOTIONS VERSUS REACTING

To communicate constructively with their child, parents must genuinely want to hear what the child has to say. All too often, parents do not really want to listen to their child explore his feelings. They want the child to listen to *their* feelings about his situation, give up his feelings and adopt theirs, and apply their solution to his problems. When he resists doing so, it can be very difficult for them to keep from reacting anxiously or angrily. But the more upset parents become, the less secure is the base that they provide and the more they interfere with the child's ability to invest in school. In all too many families, parents' efforts to communicate with their underachiever deteriorate into a shouting match or a standoff. And the child's belief that there is no comfort or help to be had anywhere, even at home, is further solidified.

"I don't remember what my dad said about my report card," said one seventh-grade boy mournfully, "but he sure said it for a long time."

Parents can even become trapped into believing that anger is the only effective way of communicating with the underachiever. As one frustrated parent remarked, "The only thing that seems to work is getting mad." Indeed, in the short run, the underachiever may work harder to try to avoid his parents' anger. But in the long run, threats cannot produce the kind of internal transformation that is required for the underachiever to become an achiever, and they only confirm his belief that other people can't help him.

"I like it here," commented Elvin, an eight-year-old second grader, as we sat together in my office. "You don't yell." He paused for a moment and then added hopefully, "Can you tell my parents to use soft voices?"

Managing emotions does not imply that parents should never get angry. It means expressing their concerns in such a way that the child feels cared for and supported rather than criticized. And that takes practice.

REACTING: *Sally, that's the third time this week you've forgotten to bring your books home. What's the matter with you? If you don't bring your books home tomorrow, you're grounded for a week!*

MANAGING EMOTIONS: *Sally, I am very concerned about your forgetting to bring your school materials home so you can do your assignments. What do you think would help you to remember?*

REACTING: *Marvin, are you deaf? I've told you three times to turn off that TV and get going on your homework!*

MANAGING EMOTIONS: *Marvin, I get upset when I see that you are not keeping to the study time you chose. This is home-work time, not TV time.*

CONSTRUCTIVE COMMUNICATION STRATEGY 3:
INVITING VERSUS INTERROGATING

PARENT: *What did you do at school today?*
CHILD: *Nothing.*
PARENT: *How's everything going?*
CHILD: *Fine.*
PARENT: *Why don't you ever talk about school?*
CHILD: *I don't know. C'mon, just leave me alone, OK?*

When parents ask the underachiever questions about school, they expect to receive answers that provide information and make sense. They seldom get what they expect. In fact, the underachiever makes strenuous efforts to avoid answering questions about school, fearing that an answer implying that things are less than perfect will be met with criticism, disappointment, or some other anxiety-provoking re-sponse. Instead, he responds with denial ("Everything's fine"), avoid-ance ("Nothing's going on"), or defiance ("Just get off my back!"). All too often, parents' well-meaning questions lead to an impasse rather than a genuine dialogue with the child.

This cycle of destructive questioning, once set in motion, tends to perpetuate itself. Questioning the child temporarily reduces the par-ents' anxiety by making them feel that they are at least doing some-thing to try to help him, so they keep on asking questions. But questioning that lacks an understanding of the underachiever's internal world causes him to withdraw further. In response to his distancing, the parents press harder for information and explanations, and the vicious circle is complete.

Impossible Questions

"Why did you put off your essay until the day before it's due?"

"Do you want to fail seventh grade?"

"How could you be flunking German and not let us know?"

In their desperate effort to discover why their bright child is not doing his work, parents of the underachiever are likely to ask him impossible questions. An *impossible question* is a question for which there is no answer that would be acceptable to the person asking it *and* to the person being asked. In fact, impossible questions are actually accusations disguised as questions. The real question contained in an impossible question is, "How in the world can you have possibly thought, felt, or acted so wrongly?" When parents ask the child impossible questions, they don't want an answer. They want a promise to do better. Impossible questions make the underachiever feel more inadequate and isolated than ever. Unable to explain his behavior, he responds with excuses, silence, or a destructive communication of his own: "I don't care."

Inviting

Instead of interrogating the underachiever, parents can practice the art of *inviting*. Questioning that invites not only helps parents learn more about what's going on at school, but, more important, lets the underachiever know that they are truly interested in understanding his feelings and helping him find his own answers to his problems.

Open versus closed questions. Inviting questioning uses open rather than closed questions. An *open question* is one that cannot be answered by *yes* or *no* and allows the child to respond with a wide range of answers. Because open questions offer an invitation rather than issue a command, they encourage the child to respond not just to the question but to the communication process itself. Open questions begin with words like *what, how,* and *could:*

"What *was the field trip to the museum like?*"

"How *can your mother and I help you with your essay?*"

"Could *you tell me about your ideas for your science project?*"

In contrast, a *closed question* is one that can be answered with *yes* or *no* and so restricts the range of possible responses. Closed questions typically begin with such words as *are, have,* and *do.* Unfortunately, the questions underachievers are most likely to hear from their parents are closed questions, because parents really want to hear only one particular answer. Some examples of closed questions and the answers parents are hoping to hear follow:

"Are *you keeping up with your spelling?*" (Yes)

"Have *you done your homework?*" (Yes)

"Did *you have a good day in school?*" (Yes)

To keep questioning constructive rather than destructive, parents can practice restating closed questions in open form:

CLOSED: *Do you need help with your project?*
OPEN: *How can we help you with your project?*

CLOSED: *Did you learn anything in math today?*
OPEN: *What kinds of things are you studying in math?*

CLOSED: *Are you doing any better in spelling yet?*
OPEN: *Can you tell me how spelling is going these days?*

By inviting rather than demanding communication, the open question demonstrates that parents are interested in what the child is doing and how he is feeling but does so without criticizing or interrogating the child. Paradoxically, because it is the least demanding type of question, it is more likely than any other to get a meaningful answer.

Constructive Communication Strategy 4: Promoting Problem Solving Versus Giving Advice

CHILD: *I'm going to get a D in math.*

PARENT: *A D in math? You need to pay attention and study harder. If you don't get on the ball, you're going to fail sixth grade!*

Anxious parents are constantly bombarding the underachiever with advice on how to solve her problems. They advise her to listen to the teacher, study harder, write assignments down, and so on and so on. This kind of advice giving is destructive for several reasons. First, when parents supply the child with a solution to her problems, they are depriving her of the opportunity to develop her own problem-solving skills. In effect, they are telling her that she is incapable of figuring out for herself what would be most helpful, thus reinforcing her view of herself as incompetent. Second, although her parents intend to help the child become more responsible, all this advice giving actually keeps her dependent. The ultimate goal for any person is to be able to draw upon her own resources to solve problems and to ask for help when her problems are truly beyond her capacities. But if the underachiever is never given the freedom to decide when to ask for help, she cannot learn when it is appropriate to seek it.

Third, parental advice giving tends to be loaded with prophecies of doom if the underachiever doesn't take the advice. This kind of advice often takes the form of what one seventh grader called the "ditchdigger speech" after the gloomy predictions of his father:

"If you don't straighten up and start paying attention and trying harder, you'll ruin your chances for success. Instead of going to college and getting a good job, you'll have no future, and you'll end up digging ditches for a living."

Finally, giving the underachiever unasked-for advice *doesn't work*. The child has heard from her parents and teachers hundreds of times that if she pays attention in class and tries harder, her grades will improve. But the voices of her internal world drown out that well-meaning advice with their familiar chant that what she does doesn't make a difference. Besides, if her parents really believed she could solve her own problems, why would they spend hours telling her how to do just that?

CHILD: *Mrs. Simmons says if my math grades don't come up, she won't recommend me for Algebra I next year. But all my friends are going to be taking it!*

PARENT: *If you studied more instead of going to the mall all the time, you wouldn't have any problem getting into Algebra I next year. The way you're going, you'll be lucky to get into prealgebra!*

The problem with this kind of communication is not that the parent is giving bad advice. If the underachiever studies more, she *will* have a better chance of being recommended for Algebra I. But the parent's advice can't build the positive views of the self that support achievement, because the parent, not the child, came up with the answer. Instead of giving advice, parents can help the child develop her own problem-solving skills.

CHILD: *Mrs. Simmons says if my math grades don't come up, she won't recommend me for Algebra I next year. But all my friends are going to be taking it!*

PARENT: *You're kind of worried about next year's math class.*

CHILD: *I don't want to have to take dumb old prealgebra and not see my friends.*

PARENT: *Do you have any idea why your friends are being recommended for Algebra I?*

CHILD: *Oh, they're just math brains, I guess.*

PARENT: *You think they're going to be put in Algebra I because they're good at math?*

CHILD: *Yeah. But I want to take Algebra I, too!*

PARENT: *I wonder what you could do to get recommended for that class.*

CHILD: *I guess I could start going to Mrs. Simmons's extra help sessions after school on Tuesdays.*

PARENT: *That's a great idea! Sounds like you've figured out a way of helping yourself get into the class you want next year.*

CHILD: *Oh. I guess I have. Thanks, Dad.*

In this communication, the parent first *allows feelings* by identifying the child's painful emotions. Then, instead of reacting or giving advice, the parent helps the child figure out for herself why her friends are being recommended for Algebra I and what she can do to get that recommendation herself. Finally, he validates the child's efforts at problem solving.

CONSTRUCTIVE COMMUNICATION STRATEGY 5:
CONSTRUCTIVE VERSUS DESTRUCTIVE ENCOURAGEMENT

Parents of underachievers, especially chronic underachievers, often have trouble giving their children constructive encouragement. "Of course I encourage my child," parents may be protesting at this point. "I tell my child how smart he is all the time!" But because the underachiever's perceptions are filtered through his maladaptive internal belief system, sometimes what parents think is encouraging is actually discouraging to the child.

The You-Can-Do-It Speech

"Son, we know you can do better in school. You're very bright. We know it and your teachers know it. All you need to do is try harder. You can do it!"

Parents deliver hundreds of these *you-can-do-it speeches* in the effort to encourage the underachiever to do better in school. Unfortunately, when parents tell the child that they know he has the intelligence to do his work, it merely reminds him that he has failed to live up to their expectations. The message that he hears is quite different:

"You can do it. So why aren't you doing it?"

Moreover, parents usually deliver a you-can-do-it speech after the child has received a poor grade or a bad report from school, so that he is likely to associate failure and humiliation with such a speech. Instead of hearing encouragement about his *future* performance, the child hears only his parents' disappointment with his *current* performance. Besides, deep down, he believes that his parents are wrong. He doesn't believe he can do it. A little voice inside him whispers, "If I try and fail, everyone will know I'm dumb. At least now my parents think I'm smart." As a result, this kind of "encouragement" is destructive because it actually reinforces the child's lack of effort.

The Just-Do-Your-Best Speech

"Just do your best. We don't expect As."

"Just do your best. Not everybody can be a math whiz like your sister."

With the *just-do-your-best speech*, parents are trying to encourage the underachiever by assuring him that he doesn't have to be perfect to win their approval. But the underachiever's deep-seated sense of inferiority distorts the parents' message, so that all he hears is that his parents do not expect him to achieve excellence. He hears that they believe he is so incompetent that a mediocre performance is acceptable. With this kind of destructive encouragement, his view of himself as inadequate becomes more entrenched.

The Yes, But Speech

"Yes, you got a C on your math test, but you could have gotten an A or B if you'd tried."

"Yes, I'm glad you're paying more attention in Miss Silber's class, but I wish you'd started doing that last semester."

The *yes, but speech* consists of a positive statement followed by a negative statement that destroys the positive value of the first. Like the other forms of destructive encouragement, the parents' well-meaning words only strengthen the child's conviction that he has disappointed the people he most loves and wishes to please. It can be very difficult for anxious, frustrated parents to say to the underachiever with genuine enthusiasm, *"Yes,* you brought your grade in English up from a *D* to a *C!"* without adding, *"But* why didn't you bring it up to an A?" when they know the child is capable of doing better. But if the underachiever's small steps toward change are consistently devalued by this kind of "encouragement," he is likely to feel so discouraged that he stops trying to improve.

Constructive Encouragement: Encouragement in the Here and Now

Instead of using these destructive forms of encouragement, parents can use *encouragement in the here and now,* a constructive form of encouragement that reshapes the child's internal images of himself and others in more positive directions. This type of encouragement focuses not on *product* ("You know you can do better work than this") or *ability* ("We know how smart you really are") but on *effort.* Moreover, it focuses on the underachiever's present strivings, not his past failures or the terrible things that will happen to him in the future if he doesn't shape up. Encouragement in the here and now uses such phrases as *you are working hard on* and *you are learning to.*

"You are really working hard *on those spelling words."*

"I can see that you are learning *to get the hang of word problems."*

"You're really sticking to *your study schedule."*

This type of encouragement supplies powerful motivational fuel to the underachiever for several reasons. First, it is genuine. It does not deny the reality that the underachiever's present performance leaves much to be desired by telling him untruthfully how well he is doing now. Nor does it reinforce his sense of inadequacy by reminding him of how well he could do if he just tried harder. Instead, by validating the steps he is currently taking to master a task, encouragement in the here and now helps the child see for himself the connection between his efforts and positive results.

When parents use encouragement in the here and now to support the child's attempts to do his schoolwork, the child will come to associate that work with positive parental attention and feelings of competency, a potent combination. A child who regularly receives encouragement in the here and now when he is doing his homework will begin to think of homework as something that brings him closeness with his parents and good feelings about himself. Over time, he will internalize that encouragement, and when he is faced with obstacles in the classroom or in his studies at home, that inner fuel will help him persist, even when his parents are not physically present.

OPENING THE DOOR TO CHANGE

As parents become more aware of the real meaning beneath the underachiever's mystifying and irritating language, they can use constructive communication strategies to open the door to change. By allowing the child to express his fears and frustrations about his school performance and providing support for his efforts to solve his own problems, parents can help the underachiever modify his view of himself as unlovable and incompetent and his view of others as unresponsive and unhelpful in more positive directions. When a child knows that he can truly communicate with his parents, regardless of how bad he feels, his painful emotions lose their power to bind his energy, and he is free to become an eager and enthusiastic learner.

7.

The Homework Trap and How to Get Out of It

PARENT: *Do you have any homework?*
CHILD (*pick one*): *I did it at school.*
                 I'll do it later.
                 No.

Every night, the parents of the underachiever ask the same questions about homework. And every night they get the same kind of evasions and denials. The more they try to help the child with his homework, the more she resists. The parents have fallen into the homework trap. How does this happen?

HOW PARENTS FALL INTO THE HOMEWORK TRAP

THE INSECURE PARENT AND HOMEWORK

Parents who have had trouble finding a secure base for themselves may become overly involved with their child in an unconscious effort to satisfy those unmet needs for comfort and nurturance. When the child goes to school, they miss their special relationship with the child and all the pleasures of feeling needed and appreciated by him. Because mothers are usually the primary caretakers for children, they are especially likely to fall into this trap. Homework becomes a way in which the mother can continue caring for the child. Although she is consciously trying to help the child become more independent, the enmeshed relationship continues, with homework as its focus. For all her complaints about having to manage the child's schoolwork, the mother unconsciously cherishes this means of keeping the child close.

Because of her ambivalence about her child's growing up, the mother unconsciously sends conflicting signals during homework time. She may offer so much help that she becomes intrusive and then is surprised and hurt when the child rejects her assistance. Or she may tell the child that his homework is his own responsibility but then check on his progress so often that he becomes resistant in an effort to ward off his mother's interruptions. It's important to remember that a child responds not so much to his parents' words as to his parents' unconscious feelings. So the underachiever tunes out his mother's conscious encouragement to do his work on his own but picks up her unconscious ambivalence about the child's growing up. Sensing her conflict, the child unconsciously seeks to prove to his mother and himself that he is still dependent and coerces her into helping him. At the same time, however, he wants very much to grow up, so his dependency takes on a hostile flavor. Most of the homework time is devoted not to doing homework but to waging the battle between dependence and independence, with the real nature of the struggle outside the awareness of either party.

"I don't know how to do this!" wails Max, putting his head down on the kitchen table. "Mom, you've got to help me!"

His mother hurriedly dries her hands on the dish towel and rushes over to his side. "Now, honey, what don't you understand about your spelling?" she asks.

"Everything!" Max complains. "I hate this dumb stuff."

"Max, don't talk like that. Let's see what you're supposed to do," coaxes his mother, irritation creeping into her voice as she sits down beside him. Sinking down into his chair, Max sighs heavily and averts his eyes from the page.

The Unvalidated Parent and Homework

The other type of parent who is likely to fall into the homework trap is one whose own family has failed to acknowledge his achievements at home, at school, or both. Deprived of the approval of his own parents, this parent, often the father, vows that his child will shine at school and earn the validation from others that the parent himself missed. As usual, the child responds primarily to the parent's unconscious message rather than to his actual words. Although the father urges the child to try, the child senses his unconscious need for approval and responds by becoming less and less competent at school so the father can feel more and more helpful at home.

As the child becomes less capable, the father takes over more of the task of managing her schoolwork. For this parent, the path from helping the child with homework to actually doing it for her is direct—and short. When the child announces that something important is due the next day, for example, the father may say to himself, "It won't hurt just this once to do it for her." So the father gives the child the answers to problems, supplies ideas for creative writing assignments, and so on. The child is grateful, the father feels appreciated, and the homework gets turned in on time.

But this kind of help cannot build the feelings of competence that will lead to future achievement. Quite the contrary—the effects of such "helping" are destructive. A parent who yields to the temptation to save his child from the logical consequences of her own actions is depriving her of learning the invaluable lesson that actions (and inaction) have consequences in real life—precisely the message that the underachiever has failed to internalize. The child who is rescued from her homework once is likely to need to be rescued again and again. Even more damaging, the child learns that deep down, behind her father's protestations of "I know you can do it!" her own parent believes that she is incapable of performing satisfactorily. If her father didn't believe that the child was incompetent, why would he take such an active role in her homework, which father and child know full well is supposed to be the child's independent work?

A son of intelligent, well-educated parents had difficulty with creative-writing assignments early in his school years. When the boy complained that he didn't know what to write, the father would supply not only the idea but also the structure for the homework. As time went on, the father continued to help, often taking over the task and dictating assignments nearly word for word. Although the boy's homework earned him good grades, he was unable to use his teachers' approval to build self-esteem because he knew the validation he received rightly belonged to his father. In fact, the boy came to believe that he was unable to write anything worthwhile on his own. The father's intrusiveness caused a minor problem to develop into a severe writing inhibition.

GETTING OUT OF THE HOMEWORK TRAP

"But I can't let Christy do her homework on her own!" protested her father. "If I don't keep on her, either she won't do it at all, or she'll rush through it and just put anything down on the paper."

To parents caught in the homework trap, there seem to be only two alternatives: managing the child's homework or leaving her to her own devices—and to failure. Their fears are understandable. But if parents continue their overinvolvement with the underachiever's homework, she will never learn to function effectively on her own. The following seven strategies are designed to help the child become an achiever at school by creating an environment at home that supports independent effort and persistence.

HOME STRATEGY 1:
INCREASING PREDICTABILITY AT HOME

"I'm always the one who ends up helping Nathan with his homework," sighed Mrs. Franklin, glancing at her ten-year-old son, who was sitting glumly in a chair in the corner of my office. "I really think he's at the point where his father ought to take over, but Daniel's hours are so

crazy that I never know when he's coming home from work." She heaved another sigh, and Nathan sank lower in his chair.

The first step in helping the underachiever deal effectively with his homework is creating a secure home environment that encourages independent effort but also offers comfort, sharing, or assistance when he needs it. Secure environments are predictable environments. Events, things, and people, while not perfectly predictable, have a certain regularity in terms of when they happen, where they are, or how they behave. Although today's parents must juggle many conflicting demands for their time and attention, the way in which they deal with those multiple demands can create an atmosphere of calm or one of disorder. Unfortunately, in some families, lack of predictability is equated with uniqueness or creativity.

Mrs. McClennan, the mother of a very bright and very underachieving seventh-grade daughter, threw up her hands in mock desperation. "I'm afraid our house is like a three-ring circus! We never know what we're going to do from one day to the next!" she confessed laughingly. The pride in her voice suggested that she considered the family's lack of routine a badge of specialness. Although she was concerned about her daughter's underachievement, she had trouble seeing a connection between the disorganized atmosphere at home and her daughter's failure to study systematically or to turn in homework on time.

In other families, a chaotic atmosphere may reflect marital tension and one spouse's resentment toward the other. For example, a wife who feels that her husband provides her with little emotional support or help with parenting may fail to have dinner at a regular hour or to keep the house in order. Or a husband whose wife's overly involved relationship with the underachiever has limited his chances for intimacy with either her or the child may find himself working erratic hours or traveling frequently at short notice. Unaware of the motivation behind the disorganization, the parent is not only unable to change his or her own behavior but obtains unconscious gratification from the child's lack of organization and sends signals sanctioning it.

Predictability is the foundation of a secure base. In a predictable home environment, the child is free to use his energy to explore the world of his studies rather than wonder about when to do his homework, when and what to eat, where his parents are, or what he is doing that day. All children, especially insecurely attached underachievers, want and need their lives at home to be as orderly as possible. Having a fixed homework time in a household in which nothing else is predictable is no substitute for a calm, stable environment that supports confident, anxiety-free studying.

HOME STRATEGY 2:
INCREASING PARENTAL AVAILABILITY

The second strategy in helping the underachiever at home is increasing parental availability. For most children today, the model of family life in which the child returns from school to a stay-at-home mother who stands ready to help with homework no longer holds. In two-career or single-parent families, children may be responsible for themselves after school or go directly from school to day care or a babysitter. It may be several hours after school before their parents retrieve them from child care or return home. Many of these parents prefer that children do their homework before they arrive home, leaving the evening free for family time without the hassles of homework. For parents already coping with a career and perhaps a stressful commute as well, having to deal with homework, especially in the case of the resistant underachiever, can seem too much to bear. For their part, children often want to get their homework over with before their parents arrive to avoid any arguments about doing it or doing it the way the parents want. If, however, they have problems with their assignments, they may have no one to turn to for help or comfort. Moreover, if the parents require the child to complete his homework before they come home and on their arrival ask, "Did you do your homework?" the child is likely to hear that question as, "Have you taken care of your schoolwork so that we don't have to be bothered with it?" Such a situation does nothing to increase the child's investment in his homework. On the contrary, he is likely to do his homework hastily or not at all.

"I've told Donnie fifty times that he should do his homework at the babysitter's so it's all done before I pick him up," Ms. Fields said angrily. "He's been telling me he's done it, and now I find out from his teacher he's been lying all this six-weeks period and hasn't done most of it!" She glared at nine-year-old Donnie, who looked away quickly and pretended to be playing with a toy car.

Supervising study times and helping the child with homework when he gets stuck are hassles for tired parents at the end of a long day. But when the child perceives that his parents see his schoolwork as so important that they make a point of being available to help him with homework, he, too, will place a high value on his assignments. For these reasons, the underachiever should be helped to choose a study time *after* the parents return home, either in the late afternoon or after dinner. In addition, most children need a break after a long sedentary day at school. Relaxing and letting off steam, preferably through some kind of outdoor physical exercise, should always precede settling back down to schoolwork.

To create an atmosphere at home that encourages the underachiever to study, his parents will need to enlist the cooperation of all family members. Although some children can go off to their bedrooms and study diligently for hours while the rest of the family enjoys a television program or video in their absence, the underachiever will require support from the entire household during the homework period. While he is studying, *all* of the televisions, stereos, and radios in the house should be turned off. Even if his younger siblings do not have homework, parents should help them find some quiet activity during that time. Setting a household limit on media entertainment during the study period creates an environment that makes it easy for the child to ask for help and for parents to offer it. Nothing makes an underachiever feel less like doing his homework than having to study while (to his mind) his parents and siblings are enjoying themselves.

"Every night I have to go off and do my homework in my bedroom, and my little sister gets to stay and watch TV with Mom and Dad!" complained ten-year-old Harry, an underachieving fifth grader. "It's not fair!"

The underachiever turns a deaf ear to his parents' protests that his younger siblings shouldn't be deprived of TV because they have no homework. When the underachiever works while his brothers and sisters play, he learns that being older means losses rather than gains, and he may resolve that not only will he give up trying to please his unfair parents, he will give up on himself as an achiever as well.

Creating a study environment that is free of entertaining distractions is much easier if parents begin setting limits on television and other media early in the child's school years. When the child is in the primary grades, parents should introduce the rule that homework takes place without the television or the radio. During study time, it's off, and that's that. If the parents themselves abide by this rule, it is much easier for the child to accept. For adolescents, however, some flexibility is needed. Although it is perfectly true that listening to music can interfere with concentration, the adolescent should be able to choose whether he wishes to study with his music on or off. Children must be helped to acquire the habit of studying without visual or auditory distractions in the elementary school years. At most, parents can suggest that teenagers turn the radio or stereo off for "thinking" kinds of homework. Trying to separate an adolescent underachiever from his music connection will only strengthen his resistance. As one ninth grader put it grimly, "My parents can take my music away, but they can't make me do my homework without it."

In addition to creating a quiet, calm study environment during homework time, parents should underscore their availability to the child by choosing some activity for themselves that they can interrupt without much difficulty, such as reading or reviewing work from the office. If the child requests help at a time when the parent is busy, the parent should set another time for helping as soon as possible. Underachievers are famous for sitting for hours over their homework and doing nothing while they wait for their parents to come to help as promised.

HOME STRATEGY 3:
HELPING THE UNDERACHIEVER GET STARTED ON HIS HOMEWORK

Sprawled across her bed, thirteen-year-old Jennifer gazes malevolently at the stack of books and notebooks awaiting her on her desk. From her perspective on the bed, the pile of homework seems enormous—English, math, science, social studies, and French. With a muttered "Yuck!" she leans over, switches on the radio on her bedside table, and closes her eyes.

As any parent of an underachiever knows, the beginning of the homework time is especially stressful for parent and child alike. Because the underachiever has difficulty committing herself to a course of action (in case she can't do it perfectly), she becomes overwhelmed at the prospect of beginning her work and shuts down before she even gets started. Just looking at the tasks that lie ahead conjures up an inner voice that warns, "I can't do it! I'll never get it done!"

Parents can help the child feel more in control by teaching her to make a homework schedule for each day. They should teach the child to look over her assignments, figure out how much time each one will take, and then write out a schedule, including breaks. This simple step makes studying much more manageable. Generally, one hour of homework time should be sufficient for elementary school students, one and a half hours for middle school students, and two to three hours for high schoolers.

To help the child change her discouraging inner voice to an encouraging internal presence, parents can model self-talk that validates each small step toward the final goal:

"First I'll write up my science lab, and then I'll get a snack, and then I'll do my English, and then I get twenty minutes of telephone time with my friends."

Parents should also teach the child to begin with the homework assignment she dislikes most and proceed to the most enjoyable. This is particularly important for the underachiever, who begins with the easiest or most structured task, such as a set of math problems, and seldom gets around to the rest of her homework, especially projects or creative-writing assignments that require a good deal of thinking and planning.

Regardless of what some books imply, no study routine can, in and of itself, cure underachievement. Predictable home environments and available, encouraging parents are much more important in creating a context of security within which the child feels safe to try to master her lessons, to make mistakes, and to learn from those mistakes. But having a regular study place and time *does* help the insecurely attached under-achiever because it makes an anxiety-provoking situation more pre-dictable. As much as possible, therefore, the study period should occur at the same time every day. In helping the child select a study time, parents should consider their own work schedules, child and adult recreational activities, and child-care arrangements. Too many extra-curricular activities—and the time required to travel to and from those activities—can severely interfere with setting up regular study times or even finding time for homework. Moreover, when parents are ex-hausted with shuttling children from one place to another, they are likely to have trouble maintaining the conditions that promote effec-tive studying. Alternative study schedules should be created for days on which after-school activities preempt the regular study period. If the child's extracurricular activities leave her so tired that she cannot do her homework well or take up so much time that homework is squeezed out of the schedule, the number of activities should be limited.

HOME STRATEGY 4:
HELPING THE UNDERACHIEVER
PERSIST WITH HOMEWORK

"I read the chapter and study for hours, *but I just don't remember the material on tests," wailed Russell, a severely underachieving sixth grader. "What's the point of studying anyway?"*

Although underachievers may *claim* they study, few have realistic notions of how much they study. Parents, too, often have a hard time determining how much and how well the underachiever is studying. Knowing that the child has spent hours in his room, supposedly doing his homework, but still gets mediocre grades, his parents may wonder if he has test anxiety, a learning disability, or an incompetent teacher who tests him on material that he has not taught sufficiently. But a careful examination of those "hours" of studying reveals a very different picture from that which the child presents. "Hours" of studying usually means studying something the underachiever thought was boring (his homework) for any amount of time from five minutes (with the radio, stereo, or television on) to an hour or more. Even underachievers who genuinely make an effort to study have trouble managing the anxiety that persisting with challenging or tedious tasks evokes. As a result, an hour of study time often turns out to be fifteen minutes of finding and eating a snack, ten minutes of pausing to watch "just a second" of television on the way back to the bedroom, ten minutes of finding the necessary school materials, ten minutes of calling a friend to find out what the assignment was, five minutes of searching the radio in the effort to hear a current favorite song, and finally ten minutes of actual study time. No wonder so few written assignments get completed and so little genuine studying occurs!

HELPING THE UNDERACHIEVER UNDERSTAND THE ASSIGNMENT

Arthur looks with distaste at his English book. He briefly scans the directions for his homework exercises and then throws down his pencil in disgust. "This is stupid!" he protests. "How am I supposed to figure out how to do this junk?"

Because the underachiever has such a limited tolerance for anxiety, he may shut down on his homework if he does not immediately understand how to do it. To help the underachiever overcome this problem, parents can use a three-part process for encouraging persistence that builds the child's self-confidence because it places the responsibility for figuring out what to do on the child, not the parent. When the child protests that he doesn't know what to do, the parent should first ask him to read the problem or the directions for the assignment aloud. Even if the underachiever protests that he knows what to do, his habit of ignoring directions makes it likely that he has only a general and imprecise idea of what to do. Often what he really needs help with is figuring out the steps that are necessary to complete the assignment, not how to perform the task itself. Second, the parent should have the child rephrase the problem or restate the directions for the task in his own words. Third, the parent should ask the child to work the sample exercises or review the sample questions that usually accompany the introduction of a new concept to verify that he has truly mastered it. Reviewing and restating the directions are especially important for written assignments and projects. Underachievers tend to interpret all but the most structured tasks in their own idiosyncratic way, especially in terms of underestimating the length required for written assignments.

PROVIDING OPPORTUNITIES FOR REFUELING

Even when the underachiever understands how to do his homework, his motivational fuel is still so low that he will need regular opportunities for refueling with his parents until he can work independently for the entire study period. Underachievers get into the habit of calling (or whining or yelling) for their parents to come and help them, whether they are at the kitchen table, upstairs in their room, or down in the basement. Anxious parents often become trapped into responding to the child's persistent cries for assistance, thus reinforcing his inappropriate ways of asking for help.

> "When I'm doing my homework in my bedroom and I get stuck on something, I holler down the stairs for Mom to come and help me," explained Lorenzo.
> "And does she come and help you?" I asked.
> "She does after I've been yelling for a while!" he answered triumphantly.

At all costs, the parent should avoid sitting with the child while he is doing his work. Sitting next to the child for brief periods is fine when the parent is helping the child to understand a new concept, but when the child is actually doing the homework, the parent's continuing presence not only prevents him from working independently but implies that he is incapable of doing his homework alone. As long as the parent stays right next to the child, the child will not learn how to persist on his own. Over time, he will come to require the parent's presence to do any work at all.

Because underachievers have trouble asking for help directly, it can be hard for parents to recognize when they need refueling. Instead of actively seeking comfort or help, the child may wander into the room where the parent is and just stand there or slump silently into a chair. Unconsciously, the child is trying to manage the anxiety triggered by the challenges of his homework by seeking closeness with the parent. If the parent does not recognize the real purpose of the child's approach, he may respond with irritation: "Are you here again? Get back in your room and finish your work!" Receiving the rejection he has unconsciously provoked, the underachiever returns angrily or dejectedly to his room and proceeds not to work.

Instead, when the underachiever approaches the parent during the homework period, the parent must recognize that the child is feeling uncertain about his own competency and is asking for the parent's help in dealing with his anxious feelings. With this new understanding, the parent can respond to the child's unspoken worries with constructive communication strategies, such as allowing feelings and promoting problem solving.

CHILD: *(Wanders into the kitchen, opens the refrigerator, and gazes at its contents without taking anything out)*

PARENT: *It seems like it's hard to get through all that homework tonight.*

CHILD: *Uh, huh. Mrs. Meechum gave us tons of math problems.*

PARENT: *Sounds like there's lots to do. Is there anything I can help you with?*

CHILD: *Nah. I just get tired of homework.*

PARENT: *I bet you do. When you get done, how about a game of chess?*

CHILD: *Great! (Goes back to bedroom)*

In addition to providing opportunities for the child to use them to refuel when he gets stuck, parents can help the child learn to refuel himself during his study time. Self-refueling for the child can include taking a brief break after finishing his homework for each subject, thus providing regular rewards through the study period. Parents should also build into the family routine an enjoyable activity after the study period, such as a read-aloud story for younger children or a choice of a special television program or a game for older children. With adolescents, a time period set aside for talking to friends on the telephone is a powerful refueler.

HOME STRATEGY 5:
HELPING THE UNDERACHIEVER WITH CREATIVE-WRITING ASSIGNMENTS AND PROJECTS

"Ray, you've had three weeks to get this poetry project done!" exclaims his distressed father. "Do you mean to tell me you haven't written any of the eight different kinds of poems yet? Don't you realize you're going to fail English this six-weeks period if you don't turn in a project?"

"Well, I'm just going to have to fail, that's all, because I can't think of anything to write about!" yells Ray and storms angrily out of the room.

Because of the underachiever's problems with persistence, she is especially likely to have trouble planning and completing creative-writing assignments and projects. In fact, the underachiever's poor grades are usually the result of her failure to complete such assignments rather than low scores on tests and quizzes. Confronted with a creative-writing assignment or project, the underachiever complains that she doesn't know what to write about or can't think of a topic and uses that as an excuse not to write anything or do the project.

To help the underachiever get started on writing assignments and projects, parents should teach her the technique of *brainstorming*. Brainstorming involves writing down all the ideas the child can think of in three to five minutes. If parents present this technique as something exciting and enjoyable, it can serve as a valuable tool for bridging the gap between the child's thoughts and "the terrible blank page," as one eighth grader put it. Parents should also teach the child to write a draft of her assignment first and then use rewriting as an opportunity to refine her ideas. Because this strategy frees the underachiever from her belief that she has to be perfect on her first attempt at a task, she is less likely to shut down in frustration.

Underachievers typically make their projects or written assignments much shorter than the assignment calls for, such as a three-sentence paragraph instead of a full page. Or instead of completing a written project with illustrations, they hand in a single drawing without any accompanying text. If parents respond to the underachiever's initial effort by saying, "You haven't written enough" when she presents it, the child is unlikely to ask them for help again. Instead, parents can label the child's product as an *evolving* one:

> "You've got a good start on your English paper. That's really coming along."

> "Your ideas on the causes of the Civil War sound interesting. I'll look forward to seeing more."

At all costs, parents must resist the temptation to edit the child's written assignments or do the project for her. As much as their intervention might improve the final product, this practice teaches the child that she is incapable of producing something acceptable without her parents' assistance and only reinforces her view of herself as incompetent.

To encourage the underachiever to proofread and refine her written assignments, parents who have a computer at home can teach their child to compose her assignments using a word-processing program. Word processing makes editing simple and fun, relieves the underachiever of the burden of handwriting and rewriting, and promotes confidence in approaching even lengthy written assignments. Here again, it is important that the child herself does the actual composition, typing and all, because parents find the temptation to edit the child's work on the computer almost irresistible. A summer typing course can be a great investment before the underachiever gets to high school. Most children enjoy learning to type because it is a highly visible "grown-up" skill, and even elementary school children, most of whom are already fascinated by computers, can learn the basics of word processing.

Helping children to become competent, enthusiastic writers should begin as soon as possible. Parents can build the child's pride in her written work by encouraging her to put her thoughts on paper from an early age. Children can be encouraged to keep a journal, write letters and thank-you notes to friends and relatives, and add comments to parents' letters. Helping the child select attractive stationery, notebooks, and journals can also enhance interest in writing.

As always, modeling, not lecturing, is the more powerful way to teach persistence. If writing is a regular and enjoyable part of family life, it will not seem burdensome to the child. One opportunity for the child to watch the parent writing and *enjoying* it is worth a hundred lectures by the parent that the child should take her writing assignments seriously. Does the child see her parents write to friends and relatives, jot down ideas for a poem, copy out recipes, or make notes for work the next day? Finally, it is not enough for one parent to write in solitude. Writing, as with reading and other forms of intellectual exploration, must increase opportunities for emotional sharing among family members if it is to have real value in the child's eyes.

HOME STRATEGY 6:
HELPING THE UNDERACHIEVER
CHECK HIS HOMEWORK

"I used to ask Dad to help me with my homework," confided fifteen-year-old Matthew. "I'd just want to know the answer to one little thing, but he'd want to look at all my answers and make me change what I had. Now I don't ask him for help anymore."

One of the main reasons why the underachiever is reluctant to ask for help with his homework is that his anxious parents tend to confuse assistance with evaluation. The teacher, not the parents, must be the final judge of the quality of the homework. Thus, as hard as it may be, parents should check the child's homework *if and only if* the child asks them to do so. Otherwise, the child will come to associate studying (and getting help from his parents) with intrusion and criticism.

> Mr. Kissler pauses for a moment at the door of his thirteen-year-old daughter's room, where she is doing her homework. "How's it going, Cammy?" he asks.
>
> "OK, I guess," is the rather uncertain answer.
>
> "Let me know if I can help with anything. I'll be down in the family room," her father offers.
>
> "Thanks, Dad. Maybe you'd have time to look over this poem when I get done?" Cammy asks tentatively.
>
> "I'd enjoy that, honey," he responds.
>
> "Thanks, Dad. I'll be down in a little while," says Cammy, now smiling, and returns to her work.

To check homework constructively, parents' communications about what needs to be corrected should be descriptive rather than evaluative. That is, parents should *describe* what needs to be changed rather than *label* the quality of the child's work.

DESTRUCTIVE CHECKING:	*This is so sloppy your teacher will never be able to read it.*
CONSTRUCTIVE CHECKING:	*I have trouble reading your answers here.*
DESTRUCTIVE CHECKING:	*This paragraph makes no sense at all. How do you expect Mrs. Stevens to know what you're talking about?*
CONSTRUCTIVE CHECKING:	*I'm not quite sure what you mean in this paragraph.*

Moreover, parents should always invite, not order, the child to correct any mistakes they find in his homework. After all, the homework is ultimately the child's responsibility, not the parent's. The parent who continually requires a child to redo his homework will eventually hear that the child has no homework.

HOME STRATEGY 7:
HELPING THE UNDERACHIEVER GET HIS HOMEWORK BACK TO SCHOOL

Mrs. Houchin stared incredulously at her daughter's fifth-grade social studies teacher. She couldn't believe what she was hearing. "Sally received an F in social studies because she only turned in two assignments this marking period," repeated Mrs. Connolly.

"But I know Sally does her homework because I see her doing it," Mrs. Houchin protested. "She sits right at the kitchen table while I fix dinner. I just don't understand it. Are you sure you didn't misplace it?"

"I'll look again," said Mrs. Connolly, "but I don't usually lose students' papers. Sally's homework just isn't getting to me." When she and Mrs. Houchin searched Sally's desk, they discovered several of the missing papers stuffed underneath her books.

Parents and teachers know all too well that underachievers often claim to lose their homework. But when parents have made a conscientious effort to supervise the child's homework, its mysterious disappearance can create hard feelings between home and school, with the distressed parent accusing the teacher of losing the papers and the confused teacher wondering if the parent is covering up for the child's failure to do the work.

How does this lost paper syndrome happen? Although teachers do misplace homework papers occasionally, a pattern of lost papers nearly always indicates that the underachiever is, once again, refusing to be helped. It's a long journey from the bedroom desk or kitchen table to the bus, then to the classroom, and finally to the teacher's desk. When a child appears to be doing his homework at home but "loses" it—which happens with underachievers far more often than either parents or teachers imagine—one of several motives may be operating. First, losing assignments may reflect the child's resentment at his parents' overmonitoring of his homework. His parents may have made him do the work, but they can't make him turn it in. The lost paper syndrome is a bitter reminder to parents that they cannot win the homework battle by force. Just as parents must rely on the child to bring his assignments (and the materials with which to do them) home, so parents must rely on the child to complete the process, even if they manage to control what occurs between those two steps.

A second motive behind the lost paper syndrome is the underachiever's fear of inadequacy. Although the child has completed, or at least attempted, the assignment, his fear of inadequacy may be so great that he cannot risk an evaluation of his efforts. This is especially likely to happen in a subject in which the child feels insecure or when the assignment is open-ended.

It should be noted that most underachievers who "lose" their papers, whether out of resentment or from fear of inadequacy, do not consciously intend to do so. Nevertheless, they manage to arrange things so that the papers disappear. Papers get lost in lockers and book bags, get "accidentally" thrown away, or get stuffed into pockets and forgotten, only to be discovered by the parent in the form of tiny shreds of paper scattered throughout the laundry. The child himself may be completely at a loss when asked to explain what happened to the assignment the parent watched him work on the night before.

Denise twisted her hands together and wrinkled up her face with puzzlement. "I know I did my science questions, but I just can't remember what happened to the paper," she protested. "I had it last night, but today in class I couldn't find it."

A few underachievers, however, are fully aware of their actions and the academic consequences of those actions. Their fear of inadequacy is so intense that they cannot risk a possible negative response to their papers, so they settle for the certainty of failure instead.

"I do my homework at home, I really do," Alan admitted. "But then I think, it's not going to be as good as the other kids', and I don't turn it in."
"What do you do with it?" I asked.

"Sometimes I just stick it in my notebook and don't give it to the teacher. Sometimes I drop it out of the bus window when the driver isn't looking," he said sheepishly.

SOLVING THE LOST PAPER SYNDROME

If the underachiever begins "losing" some or most of his homework, parents should first check for changes in the way they have been helping with homework. Losing papers may be the child's conscious or unconscious resistance to parents' setting new limits at home for studying. In that case, parents should use the constructive communication strategy of *allowing feelings* to show that they understand the child's feelings but expect him to verbalize rather than act out those feelings.

> PARENT: *Patrick, Mr. Goucher says that you've failed to turn in three homework assignments this week.*
> CHILD: *I guess they just got lost.*
> PARENT: *I'm wondering if the lost papers are your way of letting us know how you feel about our limiting television on school nights now. I know you're upset about missing some TV programs, but I'd rather you talk to your mother and me about it than forget your work and get a lower grade than you deserve.*

If, on the other hand, parents suspect that the child may be losing the papers because of fear that his work isn't good enough, they will want to communicate a message of understanding and an offer of support:

> PARENT: *It sounds like it's been hard to get your homework handed in lately.*
> CHILD: *Yeah. I just can't seem to keep track of it.*
> PARENT: *You know, sometimes kids worry that their work won't be good enough even if they do turn it in.*
> CHILD: *(Pause) Biology is hard!*

PARENT: *It sounds like it's tough going in science right now. What about if we find you some help with that?*
CHILD: *That would be awesome!*

Getting out of the homework trap with the underachiever requires patience and practice by his parents. As parents use these seven strategies to create an encouraging, predictable environment in which they are available to help but do not intrude, the underachiever will develop into an increasingly self-reliant and self-confident student. Homework time will become transformed from a parent-child battle that nobody can win to a shared journey for parent and child into the wonderful world of learning.

8.

Teaming with Teachers

In her seventh-grade social studies classroom, Miss James is reviewing Latin American geography. As she points out different countries on the map at the front of the room, she asks for volunteers to identify them. Most of her pupils are watching attentively and eagerly waving their hands to participate. In the back of the room, Morey is busily carving his initials into the top of his desk with a paper clip. Every so often he glances up and looks around guiltily to see if anyone is observing him.

After fifteen minutes of review, Miss James announces brightly, "All right, class, it's time for a pop quiz!" Although there are a few groans at this news, the students take out paper and pencil and prepare to write. At the sudden change of activity around him, Morey looks up, startled. "What's going on?" he whispers to the girl nearest him.

"We're having a pop quiz, blockhead," she whispers back. "Don't you ever listen in class?" Morey makes a face at her and begins rummaging in his desk for a pencil. Suddenly, he calls out, "Miss James, if we don't have a pencil, we don't have to take the pop quiz, right?"

An exasperated look comes over Miss James's face. "Morey, it seems like we go through this pencil thing every day. Just borrow one from someone, so we can get started."

Although communicating constructively with the underachiever is the key ingredient in the helping process, effective treatment must involve both home and school because underachievement is defined by school performance. Whether the underachiever is five or fifteen, support from teachers as well as from parents is needed to encourage him to try out more productive ways of behaving. Unfortunately, motivating students in the classroom is not as easy as it sounds. Today's teachers must cope with more and more children with learning and behavioral problems and, often, with fewer resources to do so. Moreover, when teachers try to help the underachiever, they are just as likely as parents to try to treat the symptom (the child's poor academic performance) rather than the unconscious roots of the problem.

As we have seen, underachievers seem to behave in the classroom in precisely those ways that will insure failure. They don't pay attention, they don't ask questions when they don't understand something, and they often misbehave into the bargain. "But I'm not at school," parents may be saying. "How can I get my child to pay attention, ask questions, and behave appropriately if the teacher, who is right there, can't do it?" Although parents can't be physically present in their child's classroom, with their new awareness of the maladaptive internal beliefs underlying his underachievement, they can play a vital role in helping him become more competent at school and in helping teachers support his efforts to do so.

SCHOOL STRATEGY 1:
COMMUNICATING CONSTRUCTIVELY WITH THE UNDERACHIEVER ABOUT HIS TEACHERS

Parents' communications about teachers can encourage the underachiever to invest in school by promoting a spirit of cooperation and teamwork—or they can undermine his investment by unwittingly fostering competition or hostility between home and school. For the underachiever to become an achiever, he must believe that the two most significant aspects of his life are working together in a mutually supportive, respectful relationship. When the child sees that home and school are collaborators rather than opponents, he will feel secure enough to summon up the courage to meet the challenges of his educational experiences.

OFFERING SUPPORT WITHOUT TAKING SIDES

Because he believes that he is not responsible for his own actions, the underachiever blames others for his problems and often brings home tales of unfair treatment by his teachers. For many parents of under-achievers, these terrible tales trigger memories of coming home from school with a complaint about a teacher, only to have their parents reject those complaints with, "I don't want to hear about it. Whatever the teacher did is fine with me." Now, as parents themselves, they may unconsciously try to undo their parents' failure to acknowledge their concerns by being overly sympathetic to the child and overly confrontational to the teacher when the child brings home complaints. Granted that all teachers (like all parents) fall somewhere short of perfection, most of the underachiever's tales of mean, unfair teachers are distorted by an internal world that characterizes other people as unhelpful. Moreover, the underachiever is constantly monitoring his parents' reactions, and if he perceives that his parents pay a great deal of attention to his complaints about teachers, he will come home with even more horrific stories.

> Mike stomps in the door and slings his books down with a thump on the kitchen table. "I had to miss half of PE today because of that rotten Mr. Sloane!"
>
> Looking up from unloading the dishwasher, Mrs. Anderson asks, "What did Mr. Sloane have to do with you missing PE?"
>
> "Mom, all I was doing was getting my stuff out of my desk to write my English composition, and he started yelling at me," protests Mike. "It's not fair! He's not the PE teacher, and we were playing basketball today."

What Mike has neglected to mention is his habit of taking an inordinate amount of time to get out his books, pencils, and other materials in an unconscious effort to make Mr. Sloane mad at him and so give him an excuse for not doing his work. Today, the long-suffering Mr. Sloane made him stay after class to clean out his backpack and desk, a task that took up part of Mike's physical education time.

Mrs. Anderson has several choices. She can spring to her son's defense and join the attack on the teacher:

"Mr. Sloane has no business making you miss PE like that! I've got a good mind to call that school and tell him to stick to teaching English!"

But criticizing the teacher not only hinders the development of a cooperative spirit between home and school but reinforces Mike's view of himself as helpless and irresponsible by rescuing him from the consequences of his behavior. Alternatively, Mrs. Anderson can assume that Mike has been penalized for some kind of misbehavior and jump on him:

"Well, if you did what you were supposed to be doing in English, you wouldn't miss PE! I bet you got into trouble in there and that's why he made you miss basketball! And if that helps you get your English grade up, I hope he keeps you out of PE all year!"

Although her assumption that Mike is omitting his contribution to the situation is correct, arbitrarily rejecting her son's version of the story only strengthens his view of other people as unempathic. Because Mike's irrational beliefs cause him to misinterpret other people's intentions (Mr. Sloane hates him and doesn't want him to have any fun in school) and to deny his own provocative behavior (he didn't do anything wrong), he has trouble seeing his role in the problem.

A third alternative is for Mrs. Anderson to concentrate on helping her son perceive his own actions more accurately.

MRS. ANDERSON: *It sounds like you were really disappointed at having to miss PE when you'd been looking forward to playing basketball.*

MIKE: *That's right! It's not fair!*

MRS. ANDERSON: *What got in the way of you going to PE?*

MIKE: *Oh, that dumb Mr. Sloane made me clean out my backpack and desk, and it took forever!*

MRS. ANDERSON: *It's no fun missing a class you enjoy. I wonder what you could do so you won't miss PE again.*

MIKE: *I guess I could keep my stuff organized.*

Instead of taking sides, Mrs. Anderson conveys her trust both in the teacher's good intentions and in Mike's ability to deal with the situation. By first allowing her son's feelings of disappointment at missing a favorite activity, she helps him feel supported enough to see the situation more accurately. She then helps him explore alternative behaviors so that the problem won't happen again.

SUPPORTING THE TEACHER'S COMPETENCY TO TEACH

Parents who have had painful school experiences themselves may inadvertently interfere with the development of a collaborative spirit between home and school by communicating negative messages to the underachiever about the teacher's competency. The unvalidated parent, whose own family was unable to acknowledge his accomplishments, is especially likely to get into an unconscious competition with the teacher. When the child asks for help with homework, the parent responds with a "better," "faster," or "more creative" way to accomplish the task.

> *Tywanda is hunched over the kitchen table, where she is struggling with a math assignment. "That dumb Mrs. Philips just can't explain anything," she complains to her father, who is sitting beside her. "We started with two unknowns in algebra today and everybody got confused."*
>
> *Mr. Harrison, a mathematician for a large corporation, nods his head knowingly. "I'm not surprised she can't get the idea across. The only people who go into teaching math these days are the ones who can't get a job in the private sector. Here, I'll show you a better way to solve those equations."*

Although Tywanda's father is consciously trying to be helpful, his unconscious competitiveness with the teacher is undermining her security at school. His criticism of the teacher as incompetent to teach and inferior to other mathematics professionals such as himself reinforces his daughter's perception of her teacher as unhelpful. Moreover, Mr. Harrison's need to outdo the teacher has prevented him from hearing the real message in Tywanda's complaint: that *she* is having trouble with algebra and is hoping for help without having to ask for it directly. Instead of questioning the teacher's competency, Mr. Harrison can use constructive communication strategies to help his daughter express her feelings more directly:

MR. HARRISON: *It's really frustrating to have to do an assignment when you're not sure how to go about it.*

TYWANDA: *You said it! I did fine in seventh-grade math but I feel so dumb now in algebra. I never thought it would be so hard.*

MR. HARRISON: *I'm sure Mrs. Philips would be the first to say that learning algebra is like learning a new language. It takes a while to feel like a native.*

TYWANDA: *Yeah. I get really confused sometimes.*

MR. HARRISON: *What could we do that would help you get more comfortable with algebra?*

TYWANDA: *Do you think you could go over a couple of problems with me after dinner?*

MR. HARRISON: *I'd be glad to. You know, I wonder if Mrs. Philips still has her study session after school on Tuesdays.*

TYWANDA: *Yeah, I think so. Maybe I'll stay tomorrow for that, too.*

In this example, the parent acknowledges the child's concerns but also labels the teacher as a helpful person and encourages the child to take advantage of her help. Moreover, Mr. Harrison's nonblaming attitude has made it possible for his daughter to seek his assistance, too.

SCHOOL STRATEGY 2:
COMMUNICATING WITH THE TEACHER ABOUT
THE UNDERACHIEVER

Just as parents need to communicate constructively with the under-achiever about his teachers, so they need to communicate construc-tively with the teacher about the child to create a collaborative treatment effort. If parents make it clear to the teacher that they are not blaming him for the child's predicament but greatly value his con-tributions to the treatment process, they will get more support for the child in the classroom. A teacher who does not have to be continually on guard against parental accusations or emotional outbursts has more energy available for supporting the child in attempting new challenges. For this reason, it is of utmost importance that parents convey to the teacher that they believe the child's underachievement is not the teacher's fault and that they support his efforts in the classroom. The more parents can support and validate the teacher, the greater his in-vestment in the child's progress will be.

As in helping the underachiever at home, building supportive rela-tionships with teachers begins with constructive communication. If parents blame the teacher for the underachiever's plight, they are likely to receive counterblaming responses in return.

PARENT: *We've tried everything we can do at home to help Roy, and now we want to know what you are going to do to help him.*

TEACHER: *I've tried everything I can think of to motivate Roy, but there's just so much I can do. I have twenty-four other students, and I can't stand over him all day long and make him work!*

PARENT: *He'd work harder if he was really being challenged in class.*

TEACHER: *Roy makes careless mistakes and doesn't do a lot of the work I give him now.*

Instead of blaming, parents can use the constructive communication strategy of *allowing feelings* and acknowledge the teacher's feelings of frustration and ineffectiveness. They can join with him by agreeing that he can't make the child work at school any more than they can make him work at home and expressing their appreciation for his previous attempts to help the child.

PARENT: *Mr. Barnes, thank you so much for taking the time to meet with us today. We'd like to talk with you about working together to help Roy be more successful at school.*

TEACHER: *I've tried everything I can think of to motivate Roy, but there's just so much I can do. I have twenty-four other students, and I can't stand over him all day long and make him work!*

PARENT: *It's difficult dealing with a child who doesn't do his work, especially when you have so many other students.*

TEACHER: *It sure is. Nothing I do seems to help Roy get his work done.*

PARENT: *We really appreciate your many efforts to help Roy. It sounds like you've tried lots of things, and you're frustrated that he hasn't responded to them. We have often felt that way at home, too.*

TEACHER: *What kinds of things did you want to try at school?*

By using constructive communication strategies, the parents have defused the teacher's defensiveness and increased his willingness to try something new in the classroom. They are now in a position to ask him to implement classroom interventions designed to help the underachiever become more successful at school. Offering suggestions to the teacher, however, can be a delicate matter. If parents come across as know-it-alls or devalue the teacher's previous attempts to help, he will resist their suggestions. Suggestions must be offered in such a way that the teacher is not made to feel that he is currently doing something wrong, but rather that certain strategies that are helping at home may be useful in the classroom. Most teachers are happy to try parents' suggestions when they are presented in the spirit of an equal partnership.

SCHOOL STRATEGY 3:
REFUELING THE UNDERACHIEVER
IN THE CLASSROOM

INCREASING TEACHER-CHILD PROXIMITY

As at home, helping the underachiever persist at school begins with increasing his opportunities to receive reassurance and encouragement from an attachment figure, which at school is the teacher. To increase refueling opportunities in the classroom, parents will first want to increase the child's promixity to the teacher. Popular lore has long supported the notion that students who sit in the front of a classroom make better grades than those who sit in the back. Although it is not clear whether more capable students choose to sit closer to the front or become more capable by sitting up front, opportunities for refueling clearly increase with increased nearness to the teacher. Since most teachers stand at the front of the room for group instruction, the child who sits in the front row has the best chance of receiving positive reinforcement for appropriate behavior and redirection for inappropriate behavior. The front of the room is also freer of distractions. Although the underachiever is a genius at finding things to distract himself, his choices are more limited if he sits in the front of the room. Instead of having a roomful of classmates to look at, he has only his neighbors on his right and left in immediate view.

If the room is arranged in groups of desks or if groups of children are seated around a common table, as is often the case in elementary school classrooms, finding an appropriate place for the underachiever is more difficult. With so many opportunities to interact and distract, concentrating on school tasks can be difficult for even the most motivated student. In such cases, parents can ask to have the child seated next to quiet, high-achieving children and as near to the teacher as possible. It also never hurts to ask the teacher if she would consider arranging the desks in rows instead of groups. Teachers often get into a habit of arranging their pupils' desks the same way from year to year without considering that the physical arrangement of their classroom may be contributing to misbehavior or low achievement.

Because teachers often put disruptive students next to them to make disciplining them easier, it is important that sitting near the teacher be viewed by both teacher and child as a privilege, not a penalty. More encouragement, not more reprimands, should be the consequence of such a move. In addition, the child's desk should not be isolated from the other students' desks. In such cases, proximity to the teacher implies that the child is so "dumb" or "bad" that he cannot join the others. In and of itself, sitting near the teacher cannot cure underachievement, but it can help encourage attentiveness, reduce misbehavior, and strengthen the emotional bond between child and teacher.

How Refueling in the Classroom Works

Travis sits half in, half out, of his seat in his fourth-grade classroom. He looks at the other students, out of the window—anywhere except at his arithmetic worksheet. Grading papers at her desk, Mrs. Chambers notices that he has stopped working. "Travis, please bring your paper up here," she directs. Travis shuffles up to her desk, an apprehensive expression on his face.

"Looks like you're a little stuck," she says with a smile. "How can I help?"

"I just don't get this problem," Travis confesses, pointing to his paper. Mrs. Chambers spends a few minutes reviewing it with him and gives him another warm smile.

"Thanks, Mrs. Chambers," says Travis, now also smiling. He goes back to his seat and begins working busily.

Refueling in the classroom can serve the same function as refueling during homework time. Parents should explain to the teacher that they know the child lacks motivation and they are trying to help him develop it by "refueling" him. Parents should describe how they are using refueling during homework time and request that the teacher try it at school.

"Would it be possible for you to let Rhonda come up and check in with you for a minute when she gets stuck on her work? We find that when she gets stuck during homework time, often she just needs a little reas-

surance that she's on the right track. We've been trying that strategy for a while at home, and it seems to be working pretty well."

SCHOOL STRATEGY 4:
INCREASING CONSTRUCTIVE
TEACHER-CHILD INTERACTIONS

Another strategy that helps the underachiever modify the maladaptive internal perspectives that are interfering with her ability to learn is to create additional opportunities for her to interact constructively with the teacher. Because the underachiever anticipates that others will be unhelpful and acts in such a way that they tend to reject her, she benefits from a chance to spend time with the teacher outside their problematic interactions in the classroom. On a one-to-one basis, she has an opportunity to transform her distorted view of the teacher as someone who is uncaring and critical into a view of someone who is genuinely concerned about her and supportive of her efforts to achieve.

Six-year-old Lily refused to read in her first-grade classroom. When her teacher asked her to participate in her reading group, she would either sit mutely or avert her eyes from the page and attempt to recite the passage from memory. As time went on, she completed less and less work and quarreled more and more with her classmates. When her mother tried to help her with reading at home, Lily was so resistant that every night became a battle. In desperation, her mother and teacher agreed that Lily would stay after school two days a week to receive individual help in reading from the teacher.

Within a month, Lily was participating enthusiastically in her reading group. She seemed happier and was getting along better with the other children. With renewed confidence in her own ability and the willingness of others to help her, Lily began permitting her mother to work with her at home as well. Both mother and teacher reported steady improvement throughout the year.

At the middle and high school levels, the after-school "help sessions" that many teachers offer can be equally constructive. Because underachievers seldom ask parents' permission to attend these sessions (or inform parents that such sessions exist!), parents may need to contact teachers to find out what kind of assistance is available and then actively encourage the child to attend. Mathematics, foreign language, and science teachers are especially likely to offer this kind of help. In the supportive, informal atmosphere of these one-to-one or small-group situations, the underachiever's image of the teacher as inaccessible and unhelpful gradually becomes modified in more realistic, positive directions. At the same time, the additional contact helps the teacher change her perception of the child. Gratified that the child showed enough interest to seek extra help (even if the parent is the motivating force at first), the teacher begins to modify her image of the underachiever as unmotivated and irresponsible.

Bounding through the school library at breakneck speed, Martin pulled up short when he saw me. "I'm on my way to Mr. Carson's geometry help class," he explained between breaths.

"So how's that going?" I asked, remembering that not too long ago, Martin had been complaining about what a "grump" Mr. Carson was and had been getting D's in his class.

"It's going OK," he reported with a grin. "Gordon's staying, too. Our moms fixed it so they take turns picking us up at four o'clock. You know, Mr. Carson's not such a bad guy when you get to know him. He just rides us about our work because he wants us to be prepared for Algebra II next year. See ya!" And with that, he raced out of sight.

SCHOOL STRATEGY 5:
HELPING THE UNDERACHIEVER LISTEN
EFFECTIVELY IN CLASS

TEACHER: *Darren, are you paying attention?*
DARREN: *(Who has been gazing out of the window) Huh?*

TEACHER: *Darren, what page are we on in our math book?*
DARREN: *(Mumbling) I don't know.*
TEACHER: *Darren, if you don't start listening in class, you'll have*
            no idea how to do your homework.
DARREN: *(Inaudible)*

The underachiever has trouble paying attention for many of the same reasons that he has trouble doing his work. Because he believes that only a perfect performance can rescue him from his inadequacy, the prospect of failing to know something already or failing to grasp a concept immediately makes him intensely anxious. To avoid stirring up these disorganizing feelings, he *withdraws his attention* from his surroundings by daydreaming or engaging in some distracting behavior, such as playing with his materials or talking to his neighbors. Because *not* paying attention makes him less anxious, it is highly reinforcing, and over time becomes habitual.

The underachiever also does not pay attention because he wishes to avoid taking responsibility for his own learning. Unconsciously, he thinks:

"If I don't pay attention, I won't know what's going on. If I don't know what's going on, I won't be able to do this assignment that I may not be able to do perfectly. So it won't be my fault if I don't do my work because I didn't know what was going on."

Any parent who doubts the operation of this thought process need only recall the underachiever's litany of excuses for his poor performance:

"I didn't hear Mr. Jenkins say we had a test today."

"I didn't know I had to have five references for my social studies report."

"I didn't know we had any homework in science."

Finally, the underachiever's failure to pay attention derives from his firm conviction that his own actions do not make a difference. He tells himself:

"Even if I concentrate on what the teacher is saying, I still won't understand what to do. So what's the point of listening?"

Providing Opportunities for Effective Listening at Home

Helping the underachiever become a more effective listener at school begins with providing opportunities for meaningful listening experiences at home. Today, many, if not most, of a child's listening experiences outside school center on television. Unfortunately, television viewing provides little practice in the kind of active attending and listening skills required for learning in the classroom—that is, focusing on the speaker and thinking about the meaning of his message. Television also has negative effects on the development of effective listening skills because it preempts communication among family members:

"C'mon, Mom, not now, this is my favorite show!"

"Lillian, please don't stand in front of the TV when Daddy's trying to watch the news."

"Mom, tell me later during the commercial, OK?"

The majority of the time the family spends together in the evening may be taken up by a succession of television programs that blot out chances for parents and children to talk to and listen to each other. Even the morning routine in many households often includes television as a way of keeping children quiet and entertained as busy parents try to get the children off to school and get ready for their own jobs at the same time.

If parents are to help the underachiever improve his attending and listening skills, they must begin by limiting the amount of television he watches and substituting experiences that promote verbal interactions instead. Games, arts and crafts materials, and toys designed for fantasy play encourage children to express their thoughts and feelings. Books are another important resource for helping children increase their ability to pay attention and listen. In addition to reading the child the traditional bedtime story, parents can invite him to select books to read aloud to *them* or to his younger siblings. The opportunity to read to others not only builds self-esteem but promotes emotional sharing between parent and child. The child enjoys contributing something to the parent, while the parent models effective listening for the child. Introducing children to music through participation in band, school or religious choral activities, or private instruction offers other attending and listening experiences that are rewarding.

Modeling Effective Listening Skills at Home

The most powerful strategy for teaching effective listening skills, however, is letting the child experience for himself *what it feels like to be listened to*. Although parents and teachers often *tell* children to listen, their words fall on deaf ears. Expecting a child who is having trouble listening in the classroom to listen to a lecture about why he should listen more in class violates common sense.

PARENT: *Johnny, Miss Peterson says you need to listen more in her math class. She says you could do much better if you just paid more attention.*

CHILD: *But Dad, that class is so boring.*

PARENT: *Well, it wouldn't be so boring if you paid attention to what was going on. Don't you know how important math is for your future?*

Instead of telling children to listen, parents can *show* children what it is like to be genuinely listened to. Being lectured about listening and being listened to by an interested, caring person could not be two more different experiences.

PARENT: *Johnny, Miss Peterson says you need to listen more in her math class. She says you could do much better if you just paid more attention.*

CHILD: *But Dad, that class is so boring.*

PARENT: *Paying attention can be hard when the subject doesn't seem very interesting.*

CHILD: *Yeah. Besides, she's got me stuck behind that nerd Roger, and he runs his mouth the entire period.*

PARENT: *Roger talks a lot in class, huh?*

CHILD: *He sure does. He thinks he's such a hot shot in math because his dad's an accountant. His father probably does all of his homework for him.*

PARENT: *Sometimes a little extra help in math can really help with the rough spots.*

CHILD: *I wish I had somebody to help me like dumb old Roger does.*

PARENT: *I think getting some help for you is a great idea. How about asking Miss Peterson for some suggestions for a tutor for you?*

CHILD: *Sounds good to me!*

Here, the parent is modeling the kind of active, attentive listening that will help the child become more successful in the classroom. Moreover, by managing his emotions so that he can really listen to the child, the parent is able to understand the true nature of his concerns. He learns that Johnny is tuning out math because he does not understand what is going on in class. He also learns that sitting next to a high achiever is making his son feel even more incompetent. Through effective listening, he helps Johnny express his wish for help and then responds in a way that supports him in solving his own problem. With this strategy, the child experiences for himself that listening effectively can have positive results.

SCHOOL STRATEGY 6:
HELPING THE UNDERACHIEVER
ASK EFFECTIVE QUESTIONS

*"Sean, how could you get a D-minus on your science project? What
happened?" exclaims his distressed mother.*

*"I didn't understand what Mrs. Gaston wanted us to do, I guess,"
mumbles Sean.*

*"Well, if you didn't understand what she wanted you to do, for
heaven's sake, why didn't you ask her?" his mother asks exasperatedly.*

*Sean shrugs his shoulders. "I don't know," is his nearly inaudible
answer.*

The underachiever's questioning takes one of two equally unhelpful
forms: either she asks no questions or she asks ineffective questions. If
she fails to understand something in class but doesn't ask any questions,
the teacher has no way of knowing that his presentation has missed its
audience. As time goes on, the child's confusion becomes cumulative,
especially in subjects like reading and mathematics in which the acqui-
sition of basic skills and concepts is fundamental to subsequent learning. Unfortunately, the longer her confusion exists, the less likely is the
underachiever to let the teacher know that she is in trouble. Admitting
that she doesn't understand something would only intensify her feelings of inadequacy. Moreover, she fears that her questions will be
greeted with questions by the teacher for which *she* has no answer:

"Haven't you been paying attention?"

"Why didn't you ask that earlier?"

*"Where on earth have you been this semester that you don't know
that?"*

That other students ask questions and get answers does not encourage her to do the same because her internal world predicts that *her* requests for assistance will meet with a negative reaction. So she conceals

her lack of understanding, tunes out more and more instruction, and falls farther and farther behind.

Types of Ineffective Questions

The underachiever's ineffective questions fall into several categories. The first type is *inattentive questions*. These questions are ineffective because the child simply has not been paying attention. In fact, she has been busy *not* paying attention by playing with her materials, talking to classmates, or just "fuzzing out," as one seventh-grade boy put it. As the classroom comes back in focus, she suddenly realizes she has no idea what's going on and blurts out a question in a desperate effort to find out what she's missed. As a result, her questions are either unrelated to the topic at hand or have just been asked by other students. The teacher usually greets the inattentive question with the response, "Haven't you been listening?"

The second type of question asked by underachievers is unconsciously designed not so much to seek information as to express resistance. *Resistant questions* are not questions—they are complaints:

"Do we have to write in complete sentences?"

"Do we have to put a heading on our papers?"

"Are we supposed to outline the chapter?"

Because the teacher recognizes the real meaning of these questions, he tends to respond in a rejecting manner:

"I just answered that!"

"Yes, you certainly do have to do that."

Third, the underachiever asks questions to express helplessness. The *helpless question* is by far the most frequent type of underachiever question and is phrased not as a question but as a statement:

"I don't understand!"

"I don't know how you got that!"

"I just don't get it!"

Instead of asking something specific ("How did you get *sixteen* as a remainder?"), the helpless question takes the burden of responsibility for learning from the child and places it squarely on the teacher. The helpless question is not only a reflection of the underachiever's belief in her own incompetence, it is also an accusation. It is the teacher's fault that she doesn't understand what to do. Because the helpless question doesn't ask anything specific, the teacher has no way of knowing what it is that the underachiever doesn't understand. Moreover, because the underachiever invariably asks a helpless question *after* the teacher has finished delivering a set of instructions or an entire lesson, it implicitly demands that he repeat the instructions or lesson again. If the teacher tries to focus the question by asking, "What exactly don't you understand?" the underachiever's response is, "I don't understand *anything*" or words to that effect. A few minutes of this is enough to induce the most patient teacher to respond with rejection: "How can I help you if you can't explain what you don't understand?"

The result of the underachiever's ineffective questions is that she fails to gain any information that would help improve her performance. Instead, her questions serve only to confirm her view of others as unresponsive, critical, and rejecting.

> *"I'm trying to do better in class, I really am, but Mrs. Brooks just won't call on me," eleven-year-old Janet complained. "Today I didn't understand something so I put up my hand to ask a question. I had my hand up for fifteen minutes and she didn't call on me! She just wants me to fail English!"*

As Janet describes the incident, she is the innocent seeker of information and the teacher is the malicious withholder. But when Janet's mother called the teacher, the teacher painted a very different picture.

"Certainly I didn't call on Janet," retorted Mrs. Brooks. "I had ex-plained the classwork thoroughly and provided time for questions, and she hadn't been paying attention. It happens all the time! And when I wouldn't call on her, she huffed and puffed and slammed her book down on her desk and refused to even try to do any of the exercises!"

Just as telling underachievers to listen won't make them more atten-tive, so telling them to ask questions when they don't understand what to do won't change their questioning behavior. Instead, parents will need to let them experience for themselves that asking for help can be truly helpful.

Encouraging Effective Questioning

Parents whose questions met with criticism or rejection by their own parents are likely to have trouble responding to their own child's ques-tions empathically.

History textbook in hand, Shelia approaches her mother, who is folding laundry on the bed. "Mom, what's a 'crusade'?"

"You've never heard of the Crusades?" asks her mother in a shocked voice. "I'm surprised! The Crusades came about because . . ." She fails to notice that Shelia, an abashed look on her face, is beginning to edge away.

If home is not a safe place where the underachiever can risk any question, even a "dumb" question, she is unlikely to ask questions in the classroom and expose her ignorance to her teacher and peers. In-stead, parents can encourage the underachiever to ask effective ques-tions by making it clear that asking questions is acceptable in the family and that nobody is expected to know everything.

History textbook in hand, Shelia approaches her mother, who is folding laundry on the bed. "Mom, what's a 'crusade'?"

"A 'crusade'? That's a good question. Let's see if we can find the answer in your book," suggests her mother, patting the bed beside her in

*a invitation to join her. "What about checking the glossary in the
back?"*

Second, when the underachiever asks ineffective questions at home,
parents can shape her questions in more useful directions.

CHILD: *I don't understand any of this dumb social studies.*
PARENT: *It's hard for me to help you when you don't give me more in-
         formation about what it is exactly that you're stuck on.*

Such a response conveys to the child that the parent wants to help
but can't because of the way in which the child is expressing her need
for assistance. Moreover, it describes a way in which the child can get
help if she really wants it. Because the parent has managed his feelings
rather than reacted to the child's provocative "question," the child feels
supported enough to tell the parent just what it is that she doesn't understand.

CHILD: *Why do we have to do a social studies project anyway?*
PARENT: *I guess you don't feel like doing your project right now. I
         wonder if you're really ready for me to help you with it yet.*
CHILD: *I get so tired of homework.*
PARENT: *Homework can get tiresome, especially when there are
         things you're not quite sure of.*
CHILD: *Yeah. Can you go over this longitude and latitude stuff with
         me again?*

SCHOOL STRATEGY 7:
HELPING THE UNDERACHIEVER
REMEDY SKILL DEFICITS

Although the strategies outlined above will increase the underachiever's ability to pay attention and sustain effort in class, parents
should also consider whether he may have major skill deficiencies that

will need additional interventions. Trying harder won't result in higher grades if the underachiever lacks the skills and knowledge necessary for success at his grade placement. Especially for older underachievers, the years of inattentiveness, ineffective questioning, and failure to complete classwork and homework are likely to have taken their toll on important academic competencies.

In the past, underachievers with skill deficits were often retained in an attempt to help them catch up with their classmates. Because being held back in a grade cannot build positive views of the self or others (usually quite the contrary!), retention is not an effective treatment for underachievers who have fallen behind their peers. Instead of having the underachiever with skill deficits retained, parents should consider having him tutored. Tutoring can not only help the underachiever catch up academically but also increase his confidence in approaching challenging tasks at school.

At this point, parents may be thinking, "I'll sit down with my child every night after dinner and make sure he knows his math facts." Although parents play a vital role in encouraging achievement at home and school, they should not try to tutor their own child. The underachiever's fragile self-esteem makes it hard for him to take risks in the classroom, let alone in front of the parents whom he loves and longs to please. For their part, parents' emotional investment in the child and their pent-up frustration with his poor performance make it difficult for them to serve as nonanxious, encouraging tutors. Finally, it is a small step from tutoring the underachiever to doing his homework for him. The parents' wish for the child to improve may be so great that what begins as tutoring becomes a full-scale, permanent intrusion into his homework. For these reasons, parents who believe that their child has academic deficiencies should seek help from someone outside the home.

Finding a Tutor

Parents should begin by asking school personnel, such as the child's teacher, counselor, and principal; other parents; and PTA officers for recommendations for tutors. In large cities, options include commercial tutoring agencies, private schools that offer tutoring to nonstudents for a fee, and educational diagnostic and remediation centers associated with university teacher-training departments. Although the last of these options is an excellent, relatively low-cost choice, waiting lists for tutoring may be long. Parents may also wish to contact the education department directly for tutoring referrals. Many undergraduate and graduate students offer tutoring to school-age children as well as their peers, often at very reasonable rates.

Parents who consider commercial tutoring agencies should be cautious. Although some agencies train their employees conscientiously and provide excellent services, others engage in questionable practices. For example, some tutoring agencies administer a battery of tests as part of the intake process and to identify the child's areas of weakness. These tests may be outdated or inappropriate and provide less useful information about the child's achievement than the standardized testing data already available in his school record. After tutoring, the child is tested, often on the identical test. The agencies then use the improvement on the second testing to claim positive results. Any improvement may be due to so-called *practice effects*, in which the child's familiarity with the test artificially raises his score. Parents should also remember that contrary to the claims of some agencies, it is very difficult to improve global skills such as reading comprehension or mathematical reasoning in a short time. If an agency guarantees that the child will gain two years in reading comprehension or mathematics reasoning, for example, parents should be wary. The gains may be due to the use of outdated tests, teaching only what prepares the child for the test, or other questionable practices.

As convenient as it may be for the parents, tutoring should not occur in the underachiever's home. A different environment gives the child the freedom to experiment and make mistakes away from the anxiously watchful eyes of his parents. Parents should also ask the tutor to contact the child's teachers to obtain firsthand information about the skills in need of remediation. Regular tutor-teacher contacts should continue throughout the tutoring process.

PREPARING THE UNDERACHIEVER FOR TUTORING

As much as possible, the underachiever should be an eager (or at least willing) participant in tutoring. Parents should be aware that adolescent underachievers may be so resistant to any form of help that they will not accept tutoring until parents have been using the other strategies outlined in this book for some time.

> Mr. Sampson's voice was buoyant over the phone. "Well, we've got Cabell all set for the summer. He's going to be attending the Study Skills Center one hour a week for reading, he'll work with last year's math teacher one hour a week to catch up on his math skills, and in the morning he'll be going to summer school so he can get his English credit and go to tenth grade."
>
> "That seems like a lot of tutoring," I ventured cautiously. "How does Cabell feel about all of this?"
>
> "Oh, he says he'll go to summer school but he doesn't want any tutoring," replied Mr. Sampson. "I'm not worried about it. He'll come around."
>
> Mr. Sampson's next call, one week later, was much less upbeat. Although Cabell was attending summer school, he had flatly refused to go to tutoring.

In contrast, when parents can help the underachiever view tutoring as a support rather than as a penalty, and when it occurs as part of a comprehensive treatment program, it can be well worth the time and money invested.

> Mrs. Honig was beaming as she came into my office. "I just can't tell you how pleased we are with Barbara's tutor. Barbara loves going to see her and is doing much better in class. She says she used to panic when she didn't understand something the teacher said, but now she feels less shy about asking questions."

SCHOOL STRATEGY 8:
PARTICIPATING CONSTRUCTIVELY IN THE
UNDERACHIEVER'S LIFE AT SCHOOL

Mrs. Byers looks up from her desk, where she is surrounded by third graders waiting to have their papers checked, to see Mrs. Murphy poking her head in the classroom door. Disentangling herself from her students, she walks to the door and inquires what she can do for Mrs. Murphy, who is fully aware that school policy does not permit unscheduled classroom visits by parents.

"Oh, I had to drop off Sarah's updated shot record, and I thought I'd just come down and look in for a minute before I left," Mrs. Murphy explains airily, thrusting her head farther in the doorway and waving at her daughter. Sarah looks up from the stack of unfinished papers on her desk and smiles plaintively at her mother, who continues to engage Mrs. Byers in conversation about her daughter's progress.

Parents of underachievers often have trouble treading the fine line between being supportive of their child's education and becoming so involved in his school life that they undermine his independence. Constructive parental participation tells the child that the parents are interested in his educational experiences. Overinvolved participation tells the child that he is incompetent and that school is not a safe place. After all, if he were competent and school were a secure base, why would his parents be monitoring so many aspects of his life there?

How can parents participate in the underachiever's life at school so that they increase rather than undermine his feelings of security? Being supportive of the child's school experiences does not require sitting in the classroom or being a regular presence in the building, just as helping with homework does not require sitting next to the child and going over his tasks item by item. It requires continuing validation of his achievements and participation in school activities that invite parent involvement. The presence of his parents at school events such as teacher conference days and open houses tells the child more powerfully than words that his parents are vitally interested in his educational development. In the case of events in which the child directly participates, such as class plays or choral productions, it is particularly important that *both* parents attend. Sole attendance by the mother sends a message that the child's achievements are not important enough to warrant the father's time and attention.

Parents may rationalize their lack of attendance at school events by saying to themselves that the child can tell them about it when he comes home, that they have other important commitments, and so on. But if validating their child's achievement is not a priority for parents, achievement will not be a top priority for the child. Fortunately, schools have become much more sensitive to the fact that many parents work outside the home during the day and schedule major events in the evening or offer both day and evening programs. Divorced parents need to attend such functions as often as possible even if they are the noncustodial parent. A child already suffering from the loss of his parent at home shouldn't have to suffer the further loss of that parent's involvement at school, although, sadly, that is often the case.

Parents can also participate positively in the child's educational experiences by serving on committees, attending PTA meetings, or helping with special events, such as plays, musical programs, field days, and science fairs. Every school has several committees that welcome parent involvement, such as textbook adoption committees, gifted and talented committees, and guidance advisory boards. Busy parents may wish to sign up for onetime events, such as serving as career resource speakers on career awareness day or sponsoring a field trip for a group of students to their workplace. This type of participation not only demonstrates the parent's interest in the child's school experiences but fosters positive identification with the world of work. Serving as a chaperone for a field trip can be a useful (if sobering) way for parents to observe firsthand how their child relates to his peers and other adults in a relatively unstructured setting. Here, however, the parent should be an observer and helper to the teacher rather than a companion to the child. This means not sitting with the child on the bus and not hovering over him during activities. Staying close to the child simply implies once again that there can be no security without proximity to the parent.

For parents of children in the elementary grades, a simple but effective way of participating in their school life is to come to school to eat lunch with them. For children of this age, having lunch with a parent who comes from home or work especially for the occasion is a genuine treat. The father's presence is particularly prized because it is so unusual. The primary grade school child anticipating such a visit will announce in class not once but several times that morning, "My dad's coming to have lunch with me today!" Many schools actively encourage this practice by offering special menus on selected days. Because elementary school lunch periods are short—generally no more than thirty minutes—the time commitment for parents who live or work nearby is minimal. Taking time off from the workplace or duties at home to share lunch with the child gives a powerful message that the parent is genuinely interested in his school activities. Moreover, it builds self-esteem because in this case, the parent is the child's guest at *his* workplace. The child gets to be the expert and show the parent how to go through the lunch line, what to choose (and what to avoid), where to sit, and how to clean up, details that seem insignificant to the parent but are of vital importance in the child's mind. For the underachiever, eating lunch at school may be the skill at which he is most competent. Performing satisfactorily in the presence of the parent and having the parent share that experience can provide some much-needed validation for the underachiever.

9.

Dealing with School Misbehavior

Arnold is a bright, underachieving sixth grader. He clowns around in class, rushes through his assignments, and then looks for ways of distracting himself and his classmates. Weary of his constant interruptions, his teacher moves him to the back of the room at a table by himself. When one of the other students turns to look at him, Arnold snarls, "What are you looking at?" and threatens to "punch him out." The teacher sends him to the principal. Arnold goes home and complains to his parents that his teacher doesn't like him.

Distrustful of his own ability and the ability of others to help him with his problems, the underachieving child is very often also a misbehaving child at school. Because he believes that what he does doesn't make a difference, he makes little effort to figure out an appropriate way of dealing with his painful feelings or what the consequences of acting out those feelings will be. Like Arnold, he unconsciously tries to provoke others to treat him as the bad and incompetent kid he thinks he is. Unfortunately, over time, his misbehavior becomes highly reinforcing because it not only provides an outlet for his feelings of shame and anger but also gains him some recognition (even if it's negative) from his teachers and peers.

THE CONSEQUENCES OF SCHOOL MISBEHAVIOR

Some underachievers exhibit mild misbehavior, such as talking too much and clowning around in the classroom. Others misbehave in a passive-aggressive way by dawdling over their work, losing materials and assignments, taking long bathroom breaks, and so on. Others are more overtly defiant, talking back to teachers, skipping school, or destroying school property. Whether the underachiever is mildly noncompliant, passive-aggressive, or downright defiant, helping her behave appropriately in school is vital for several reasons.

First, misbehavior makes it difficult for the underachiever (and her parents) to develop a positive relationship with the teacher, much less the type of teamwork critical to the treatment process. Dealing with a bright child who doesn't do her work is hard enough for any teacher, but when he must waste precious instructional time disciplining her as well, even the most saintly teacher has trouble being supportive. The lecturing, nagging, and criticism her misbehavior evokes from her teacher only reinforces her image of herself as unlovable and her image of others as rejecting.

Second, the misbehaving underachiever is likely to become increasingly isolated from her peers, or at least those who have a positive attitude toward school. The underachiever who habitually misbehaves in class soon finds that her only "friends" are misbehaving, unproductive youngsters like herself. Misbehavior is reinforced within such a peer group, further solidifying antiachievement attitudes. Finally, bringing an underachiever's misbehavior under control is an essential first step in helping her become an achiever, because her disruptive behavior interferes with her paying attention and doing her classwork.

"How can I control my child's behavior at school?" parents may wonder. "Isn't it the teacher's job to discipline students?" Certainly managing students' behavior is the teacher's job, just as encouraging achievement in the classroom is the teacher's job. But as we have seen, parents are the persons who are not only the most invested in the child but also in the best position to identify the motivation behind her misbehavior. Once they understand *why* she is misbehaving, they can then work with her teachers to develop strategies that promote positive, productive behavior in the classroom.

UNDERSTANDING THE LANGUAGE OF MISBEHAVIOR

Just as parents must understand the message behind the underachiever's verbal communications, so they must understand the language of his misbehavior if they are to help him act more effectively. If we assume that the underachiever's misbehavior is an unconscious effort to communicate something about his internal world, what is the message he is trying to convey? Let's look at some of the more common messages that underlie underachievers' misbehavior.

MISBEHAVIOR AS A DEFENSE AGAINST ANXIETY

Justin is a bright but underachieving third grader who is always getting into trouble at school. Although his behavior is fine in the classroom, he gets into fights with other students in the hall, the cafeteria, and the bathroom. His teacher tells his parents that he seems to pick fights with older boys but not the younger ones.

Because the underachiever views himself as powerless and others as unavailable, he suffers from a chronic state of anxiety. For this reason, underachievers are likely to misbehave in less structured school situations, such as the cafeteria, art or music class, recess or physical education, and during class changes. With less structure, their poorly developed ability to predict how others will behave is strained to the limit, and they react by clowning around, getting "hyper," or becoming aggressive.

Strategies for Dealing with
Misbehavior as a Defense Against Anxiety

Increase Teacher Support

To help the underachiever who is misbehaving because of anxiety, parents should alert the teacher that he will need additional support during transitions and classes that permit more physical movement. Often, simply seating the child near the teacher in less structured classes or keeping him as close to her as possible during transitions can sufficiently decrease his anxiety so that he can manage his behavior. Elementary school students benefit from being allowed to walk near the teacher in line or with a "hall buddy," a positively behaving classmate who is given the task of helping the underachiever get to and from his classes.

Increase the Underachiever's Sense of Control

To help the anxious underachiever cope with transitions at school, parents should also ask the teacher to prepare the child for the change in routine: "Class, in five minutes, it will be time to go to lunch." The teacher can then have the child recall the rules in the upcoming situation and repeat them aloud: "Walk quietly and stay in a straight line all the way to the cafeteria." Then the teacher can have the child recall the consequences of breaking the rules: "Students who run or get out of line will eat lunch at the timeout table."

Providing opportunities for the anxious underachiever to increase his sense of control in the situation that provokes the problem behavior can have prompt, dramatic effects on misbehavior:

> *Guessing that Justin's misbehavior stemmed from his anxiety in unstructured situations, his parents met with his teacher to discuss ways of helping him feel more secure. The teacher suggested that he could serve as a hall monitor to help guide students to and from the cafeteria and gymnasium. Serving as a hall monitor would be contingent on his behavior at school the day before. Within a few days, Justin's behavior*

showed a decided improvement. Being a hall monitor not only gave him more control over a situation that made him anxious but also increased his feelings of being competent.

MISBEHAVIOR AS A DEFENSE
AGAINST FEELINGS OF INADEQUACY

William is an eleven-year-old fifth grader who was retained in first grade but is still performing below grade level. He behaves fairly well in most of his classes, but during math class, he doesn't listen to directions, tries to read library books instead of following the lesson, and disturbs the other students by making strange noises. Today his father got a call from his math teacher.

"I am very upset with William's behavior today," she tells him. "He kept rocking his chair back and forth and when I asked him to stop, he kept on rocking it until it tipped over backward. And then he lay there with his eyes shut pretending to be unconscious. The class just went crazy!"

Because the underachiever's precarious sense of self is threatened by tasks he cannot master quickly and easily, he is much more likely to misbehave in classes that threaten to arouse his feelings of inadequacy. Misbehavior becomes a way of avoiding the task, or at least the appearance of being invested in the task. A vicious cycle is set into motion, in which the child learns that his disruptive behavior prevents him from being evaluated in a challenging subject. This motive for misbehavior is especially common among adolescents, as years of inattention and poor study habits finally take their toll, but it can be very difficult to detect because many parents and teachers believe that it is normal for teenagers to have little interest in school.

Careful examination of the situations in which misbehavior occurs can help parents determine whether fear of inadequacy may be promoting the underachiever's misbehavior. Misbehavior that occurs only in one or two subjects may be a clue to unrecognized academic deficits that arouse feelings of incompetence. Parents of a misbehaving under-achiever should ask all their child's teachers for a frank assessment of his behavior *and* his skill development to help evaluate this possibility.

STRATEGIES FOR DEALING WITH MISBEHAVIOR AS A DEFENSE AGAINST FEELINGS OF INADEQUACY

Remedy Academic Deficits

If parents believe that the underachiever is misbehaving to avoid ex-posing his academic skill deficits, they should consider remedial strate-gies such as tutoring, placement in a class working at a slower pace, or assistance from a school resource specialist. They may also want to re-quest a psychological evaluation to determine if the child has a learn-ing disability that is contributing to his academic deficiencies. As we have seen, underachievers are very reluctant to let their teachers and parents know when they don't understand their classwork or home-work, so they are likely to fall farther and farther behind without some kind of support.

Testing by the school's educational specialist revealed that William had never mastered his multiplication tables, so that when it came to divi-sion, he was completely at a loss. His misbehavior had been so success-ful in distracting attention from his math deficiencies that neither his parents nor his teachers had discovered his problem. After he was pro-vided with daily resource help in math, his misbehavior diminished and his math grades soared.

Overcome Helplessness by Helping Others

One of the most powerful ways of helping the underachiever feel more competent is to create situations in which he can help others. Under-achievers are so accustomed to thinking of themselves as helpless that they believe they have nothing to contribute to anyone else. Although parents constantly tell the underachiever that he has the power to help himself, their words alone cannot alter his incompetent self-image. In fact, as we have seen, their well-meaning exhortations only make him think he has disappointed them by not "doing it" and increase his sense of inadequacy—and the likelihood that he will misbehave at school. Instead, they can work with teachers to find opportunities for him to make a contribution at school and observe for himself that he is being helpful.

Kurt, a ten-year-old fifth grader, had recently transferred from another part of the state. Always something of an underachiever, he was struggling in his new placement. His grades plummeted, and he began misbehaving as well. After talking with his teachers, Kurt's parents guessed that he was feeling threatened by a heavier workload and more advanced curriculum than he had faced in his previous school. At their request, his language arts teacher arranged for him to participate in the school's peer-tutoring program and help first graders with their reading twice a week.

Two weeks later, his parents received a call from his language arts teacher. "I just have to tell you how much better Kurt is doing these days," she said excitedly. "He really loves working with the first graders. He's much more cheerful in class and his behavior has really improved. In fact, he enjoys tutoring so much that I'm using it as an incentive. I tell him he has to be on his best behavior and have all his homework in before he can tutor—and he's doing it!"

In the security of the first-grade classroom, where he was sure to know more than any of the students, Kurt began to feel less helpless and more competent. He enjoyed his special status as a tutor and the admiration he received from the younger children, who considered working with a fifth grader a privilege that gave them status. He was also warmly appreciated by the first-grade teacher, who had many pupils who needed individual help in reading. As his young charges stumbled over their words, Kurt, hardly a strong reader himself, could identify with their struggle. The lessons he learned about helping not only made him feel better about himself but made him more receptive to assistance from his own teachers.

Peer tutoring is a simple but wonderfully effective strategy for reducing misbehavior and improving academic productivity—in the tutor! The difference in feelings of self-efficacy for a child whose parents and teachers tell him he can do it and a child who has the opportunity to observe himself helping someone else is enormous. If the school doesn't have a formal peer-tutoring program, parents can request that the underachiever's teacher set up an informal arrangement with another teacher in a lower grade. Most elementary school teachers are happy to arrange peer tutoring because it has benefits for teachers as well as students!

MISBEHAVIOR AS A DEFENSE
AGAINST FEELINGS OF REJECTION

As Mrs. Charles was writing the morning's multiplication problems on the chalkboard, she heard an indignant cry: "Carl hit me!" Turning around, she found Carl, a severely underachieving and disruptive fourth grader, standing with a clenched fist over one of his classmates.

After the furious teacher sent Carl to the principal's office, the principal asked me to talk with him. In our conference, Carl spoke so softly that I had to lean close to him to hear his words.

"The other kids say they don't want me in the class anymore," he whispered falteringly. "They say I make it a bad class, and they want me to go to another teacher. Perry said it two times, so I hit him." He buried his face in his hands and wept.

Misbehavior at school may also result from the underachiever's abortive efforts to form relationships with her classmates and teachers. A child who has internalized a view of others as unhelpful tends to misinterpret the intentions and behaviors of those around her. Because she expects to be rejected, she sets up situations in which others respond to her in rejecting ways. Or she comes across as so needy and demanding that she turns off her classmates. Starved for companionship and unable to understand why her overtures are rebuffed, she lashes out angrily at her peers.

The underachiever's efforts to reach out to her major attachment figure at school—her teacher—are just as ineffective. The teacher fails to understand that behaviors such as calling out or whining or refusing to work unless he is next to her are intended to bring him close. He, too, begins spurning her bids for affection. Rejected by the one person at school with whom she most wants to be connected, the child retaliates by acting out. As time goes on, the vicious circle of provocative behavior by the child followed by rejection by the teacher becomes entrenched. Eventually, the lonely child may abandon the effort to win her teacher's approval in favor of a desperate search for something— *anything*—that will attract the attention of her classmates. Assuming the role of the class clown or rebel is frequently the child's solution to the problem of gaining some measure of validation.

STRATEGIES FOR DEALING WITH MISBEHAVIOR AS A DEFENSE AGAINST FEELINGS OF REJECTION

Increase Positive Teacher-Student Time

If parents believe that the underachiever may be misbehaving because she feels rejected by her teacher or peers, there are several strategies to help her develop more satisfying relationships at school. First, parents can work to increase the amount of positive time the child and the teacher spend together. The more time teacher and child interact outside their problematic relationship in the classroom, the more opportunities they have to modify their negative perceptions of each other. Especially with preadolescents and adolescents, providing extra time before or after school, ostensibly to help the child make up missed work or remedy skill deficits, can build a more positive teacher-student relationship that will encourage effective behavior.

Promote Positive Peer Interaction in the Classroom

Because children spend so much of their time each day at school, teachers can be invaluable in providing opportunities for the child to

develop positive peer relationships. Parents can ask the teacher to provide opportunities for the child to work cooperatively, first with one
student, and then with a small group. Working together on a task with
a partner or a small group is one of the best ways to foster positive peer
relationships. Parents can brainstorm with the teacher about building
paired and small-group activities and projects into his regular curriculum. Long-term projects are especially useful in promoting group cohe-
sion because youngsters have more opportunities to modify distorted
views of each other in more accurate and adaptive directions.

*An angry, underachieving fourth grader, Davey complained constantly
about his teacher and classmates in his weekly counseling sessions.
"Those other kids are all stupid!" he proclaimed. "Who wants to be
friends with those dopes, anyway! I keep telling Mr. Summers they're
bothering me, but he never does anything about it!"*

*As the holiday season approached, Mr. Summers announced the
parts for the annual fourth-grade play. Davey was to play the leading
role. Some of the other students protested his choice of Davey as the
lead, to which Davey retorted that he didn't want to be in the dumb old
play anyway. Mr. Summers calmly repeated that everyone would participate and that Davey would have the leading part. As rehearsals continued and the students got into the spirit of the play, Davey began to
complain less and less about his peers and teachers. Mr. Summers, who
had privately feared Davey would refuse to participate, reported that
the other children were acting more positively toward him as well. In
addition, because he was spending less time arguing with his classmates, he was completing more of his work and doing better on tests.
The play was a tremendous success, earning long and loud applause
from parents, teachers, and the rest of the school. As the fourth graders
basked in the glow of the good feelings created by a cooperative effort
that earned them so much validation, Davey's behavior and grades continued to improve.*

MISBEHAVIOR AS A DEFENSE AGAINST INCREASED DEMANDS FOR INDEPENDENT EFFORT

Mrs. Davenport wrung her hands in despair. "I don't understand why Jonathan is misbehaving at school. He loved his first-grade teacher last year, but now he says he hates second grade. Yesterday I got a note from his teacher saying that he's not doing his work and that he's disturbing the other children. She says it's as if he wants her to get angry at him! We just don't see anything like that at home."

A classroom observation and conference with his teacher confirmed that Jonathan did seem to be deliberately seeking negative attention. He made faces at the other children, burped loudly and frequently, and tattled on his classmates for the most minor offenses. If the teacher did not immediately call on him when he raised his hand, he pouted and began bothering his neighbors. "Really, he's acting just like a baby," the teacher commented. In fact, Jonathan's behavior resembled that of an angry toddler having a temper tantrum.

Sometimes parents are surprised by the teacher's reports of the underachiever's misbehavior, since they don't perceive that the child misbehaves at home. It is as if the parents and the teachers are talking about two different children. The parents wonder why the teacher can't control her students and the teacher wonders how the parents can be so tolerant of the misbehavior she feels sure must be going on at home, too. When there is a marked difference between the child's home and school behavior, the child may be reacting to the increased demands for independent effort at school. In many of today's families, children have few responsibilities for chores or otherwise contributing to the household, other than interacting with the parents when the parents are available. When the parents arrive home, they may require little or nothing from the child in order to avoid more stress at the end of a long working day. Similarly, parents who feel guilty about being away from the child for so much of the day may focus on making the few hours they spend with the child pleasant, so that the child becomes accustomed to being entertained or at least left to amuse herself when she is at home. At school, however, the expectations for attention and sustained effort are quite different—and around second grade, those expectations start increasing rapidly.

The child may also be misbehaving because she is unused to sharing adult attention. A child who has spent her life as the center of her parents' attention may be accustomed to having her needs met rapidly. Just as her parents rush to fulfill her needs at home, so at school the child wants the teacher to tell her all the answers, provide her with constant praise, and in particular, relieve her of the burden of working independently. When the teacher fails to do so, she expresses her anger and disappointment not only by shutting down academically but also by misbehaving.

Strategies for Dealing with Misbehavior as a Reaction to Increased Demands for Independent Effort

Increase Refueling Opportunities

Although refueling is helpful for all underachievers, it is essential for this kind of misbehavior because the child hasn't learned how to generate her own motivational fuel. To keep functioning, she needs frequent doses of security and validation from the teacher. Refueling serves as a booster shot that not only keeps the underachiever persisting with tedious or challenging tasks but defuses her resentment about having to work independently. Parents should ask the teacher to build in at least three refuelings per day, two in the morning during independent seatwork and one in the afternoon. In addition, they should ask that the teacher allow the child to approach him to turn in each paper or worksheet as she completes it and receive a bit of refueling rather than having to complete all her seatwork before handing it in. Although these refuelings can be quite brief, contact with a warm, encouraging teacher can make all the difference between an angry, misbehaving youngster and a happy, productive student.

Genevieve was the terror of Mrs. Carillo's third-grade classroom. Although her mother and teacher had tried everything to bring her behav-

ior under control, she was so disruptive that she was constantly being sent to the principal's office. For her part, Genevieve complained that Mrs. Carillo was picking on her and never called on her in class.

As the teacher and mother talked about the situation with me, we realized that Genevieve's misbehavior tended to occur when Mrs. Carillo was busy with reading groups in the morning and Genevieve had to work on her own. Mrs. Carillo moved Genevieve's seat so that it was very close to the reading table. From there, it was easy for her to look over at Genevieve to check on her every so often while she was working with a group. She then explained to Genevieve that she would be using a secret signal to let her know she was noticing her good behavior. When she noticed that Genevieve was behaving appropriately, she would put her finger next to her eye to show that she was seeing this wonderful behavior. Thrilled at the idea of the secret signal, Genevieve tried hard to manage her behavior. Being singled out for being good rather than for being disruptive helped her modify her view of her teacher as uncaring and unresponsive. Moreover, as she gradually brought her behavior under control, she began to see herself as more likeable and capable—as someone who deserved to be a successful student.

Support Independent Effort at Home

Parents will also need to consider carefully the differences between home and school requirements for independent effort. Does the underachiever have regular responsibilities at home for doing her schoolwork herself, caring for pets, or helping out around the house? A child who has few tasks outside school for which she is held accountable will bitterly resent her teacher's attempts to make her work for extended periods on her own, especially if she finds much of her work difficult or tedious.

When Jonathan's parents talked about his problems at school, it dawned on them that their son's babyish and demanding behavior at school reflected their low level of expectations for him at home. Although he was eight years old, he was not responsible for any regular *chores or duties. With Jonathan's input, they made a chart listing several daily chores for which he was solely responsible, with gold stars to note when he completed each chore. His parents also made a conscious effort to give him positive attention when he was doing his chores and began giving him a weekly allowance "now that he was getting to be a big boy and such a help around the house." Jonathan began taking pride in his contributions to the household, and his school behavior and grades began improving as well.*

DEALING WITH SCHOOL MISBEHAVIOR AT HOME

When twelve-year-old Michael got into a fight with Jason on the bus, Michael's mother made him stay after school to help clean up the school grounds as part of his punishment. Jason's parents protested that Jason was being unfairly treated and refused to permit him to serve his punishment. Not surprisingly, Jason continued to get into fights and was eventually suspended from the bus.

As parents understand the motivation behind the underachiever's misbehavior, they can work with his teachers to implement strategies that help him cope more effectively with his negative feelings. At the same time, however, parents must make it clear to the child that although they love and support him, they form a united front with school authorities to set appropriate limits on his behavior. This does *not* mean that parents should be required to control the child's school behavior from the home. As much as possible, penalties for school misbehavior should be exacted at school. Punishing the child at home four or five hours after the infraction makes the connection between behavior and outcome even more tenuous for the underachiever. Moreover, if the school is deprived of its ability to set and enforce limits on student behavior, it is a less secure base for the child.

After the underachiever has served his punishment for misbehavior at school, parents should follow up at home by discussing the incident with the child and helping him explore more effective ways of managing his conflicting feelings, using the constructive communication strategies outlined earlier in this book. If parents avoid mentioning the child's misbehavior, with the attitude of, "It's been handled at school," he may interpret their avoidance as sanctioning the misbehavior. For serious cases of misbehavior, such as fighting or defiance of the teacher, parents should reinforce the school's disciplinary efforts by setting up additional penalties at home to underscore to the child their resolve to help him behave appropriately. Unfortunately, parents can sometimes become caught up in the underachiever's tendency to disavow responsibility for his behavior and have difficulty supporting the school's efforts at limit setting. In fact, the underachiever often resorts to pleas or threats in an effort to coax or force his parents to rescue him from the consequences of his own behavior.

"Please don't let them kick me off the pep squad! Everybody else was smoking in the bathroom, too!"

"I can't stay after school to serve detention! I'll miss band practice!"

"If you let Mr. Samuels take ten points off my grade just because I talked a couple of times during the test, I won't do any more work in his class!"

Parents may also signal their ambivalence to the child by letting him serve his punishment but then undermining the lesson of self-responsibility by compensatory acts.

"Oh, Mark, is that you at last?" cried his mother, rushing out of the kitchen, a spatula in her hand. "I bet you're sick and tired of staying after school every day this week to serve your detention. Look, I made your favorite dessert!"

The parents' failure to support the penalties imposed by the school deprives the child of the opportunity to view either the school or the parents as a secure base. For all of his protesting, the underachiever needs and wants his parents to set limits—and to assist the school in doing so.

Conversation between two ninth-grade boys overheard in the hall:

FIRST BOY: *I heard your dad really came down on you hard about*
               fooling around in biology lab.
SECOND BOY: *Yeah. He grounded me for two weeks!*
FIRST BOY: *(Wistfully) I wish my dad cared enough about what I*
               was doing to ground me.

IF MISBEHAVIOR CONTINUES

If the underachiever's misbehavior at school does not yield to these strategies, it may be a sign of more serious emotional problems. In addition, any child who sets fires; is cruel to animals, his siblings, or other children; chronically lies or steals; is frequently destructive, even of his own possessions; or exhibits reckless, risk-taking behavior is a child in need of immediate professional help from a psychiatrist or psychologist specializing in the treatment of children.

BECOMING AN ACHIEVER

As his behavior at school improves, the underachiever will begin to feel better about himself. His increased control over his own actions provides him with a greater sense of self-efficacy and personal power. As his teachers and classmates respond to him more positively, he has more opportunities to develop satisfying relationships with others. Together, his growing feelings of competency and his expanding network of supportive people build the kind of positive internal images of himself and others that strengthen his sense of security at school and facilitate his investment in his own learning.

10.

The Transformation Process

"So if we do all these things, can you guarantee Allen will improve enough to pass fifth grade?" asked a father about his underachieving son.

Parents often ask, "How long will it take to help the underachiever become a successful student?" From the perspective presented in this book, the goal of treatment is not just higher grades. *The goal of treatment is the permanent, positive modification of maladaptive ways of thinking and behaving constructed over time that have resulted in the child's underachievement.* The length of time required to alter the underachiever's ineffective views of himself and others and the underachievement based on that distorted internal world depends on several factors.

First, the amount of time required for treatment depends on parents' capacity to find support for themselves at home, at school, and in the community in their efforts to help their child. The more support parents can obtain, the more they will be able to try out these new ways of communicating and interacting with the underachiever. Second, it depends on the amount and quality of communication between home and school, including the degree to which parents are able to involve teachers in the treatment process. Although changes in parent-child interactions are of the greatest importance in helping the underachiever, change is much more rapid when home and school function as a team. Finally, the speed of change depends on the length of time that the underachiever's maladaptive beliefs and habits have been operating. Treating a chronically underachieving high-schooler is much more difficult than treating a second grader whose underachievement is just beginning to reveal itself. Parents of older underachievers should not lose hope, however. Every underachiever is capable of positive change when the most significant figures in his life can communicate their belief in his ability to succeed and their support for his efforts to do just that.

Mrs. Brady, the eighth-grade social studies teacher, darted into the guidance office as she was taking her students to lunch. "I just have to tell you!" she gasped excitedly. "Paul has had the most wonderful week in social studies! He turned in all his homework! Can you believe it?" She beamed with delight and raced back out to catch up with her class. I could easily understand her enthusiasm. Paul had such a long-standing habit of not doing his homework that he had been recommended for retention every year that he had been in middle school. Thus far this year, his chances of making it to ninth grade had looked poor, at best.

A moment later, Mr. Simons, the eighth-grade English teacher, appeared at the door. "Do you know what's going on with Paul?" he asked. "He's turning into quite a student in my class. You should see the essay he handed in today!"

Shortly after Mr. Simons had left, Paul himself, an attractive thirteen-year-old with an unruly shock of blond hair, strode in and, grinning from ear to ear, plopped himself down in the chair opposite me.

"What's all this good news I'm hearing?" I inquired, pleased but puzzled. I had been seeing Paul and his parents in counseling for several weeks, but he had said very little, preferring to doodle with magic markers rather than talk.

"I decided to do my work," he answered simply. With another broad grin, he was out of the office and running down the hall toward the cafeteria. As I thought about the changes in Paul, I remembered how hard his parents had been working to encourage him at home. Although at first they had had little hope that he could pull his grades up enough to pass, they had persisted in their efforts to help him. I also recalled that his father had become much more actively involved in his schoolwork

*and had taken time off from his job on several occasions to meet with
me and Paul's teachers. Paul's parents had refused to give up on him.
So Paul had decided not to give up on himself.*

HOW CHANGE OCCURS

As parents begin the helping process, they should bear in mind that
higher grades are seldom the first signs of the positive changes that are
occurring within the underachiever. In fact, social behavior almost always improves before academic behavior. Typically, parents first notice
positive differences in behavior at home, especially in getting along
with others. The child argues less with his parents and siblings, initiates
interactions with family members more frequently, and seems less
moody and irritable. Next, teachers begin to report improvement in
classroom behavior. The child is more cheerful and cooperative, participates more enthusiastically in classroom activities, and accepts feedback more readily from teachers and peers alike.

Grades, especially report card grades, are last to reveal the gradual
transformation in the underachiever's internal world. This is not surprising when we remember that an entire series of behaviors (paying attention, keeping track of assignments, organizing school materials,
completing work, and handing it in) contribute to a single grade at the
end of a six- or nine-week marking period. Although the often
painfully slow pace of improvement can be difficult for parents to tolerate, persisting with the strategies outlined in this book will eventually
result in positive changes in the underachiever's grades as well. The
process of change is seldom simple or straightforward, however. As the
transformation process gradually unfolds, parents should be prepared to
recognize and deal constructively with obstacles to progress, including
obstacles within the underachiever himself.

THE UNDERACHIEVER'S RESISTANCE TO CHANGE AND HOW TO COMBAT IT

For the underachiever, altering her image of herself from incompetent to capable and her image of others from unavailable to responsive is a formidable task. Despite her conscious wishes to improve, some backsliding is to be expected. In part, backsliding may occur because parents and teachers withdraw support too soon. Believing the child is at last on the right pathway, they may breath a collective sigh of relief and direct their attention to more pressing matters. The typical rise and fall pattern of underachievers in treatment thus partly reflects the tendency of the adults helping the child to reduce their support after an initial improvement has occurred.

> Clara had been underachieving throughout her fourth-grade year. With extra support from her mother and teachers, Clara's grades improved dramatically. In fact, she succeeded in making honorable mention on her report card. Clara was thrilled. Her mother was thrilled. Her teachers were thrilled. But shortly after this success, her grades and her classroom behavior began to deteriorate.
>
> "I'm really disappointed in Clara this six weeks," her reading teacher reported to her mother. "She's been doing so much better lately, but now it seems like she's gone back to her old ways. And she's starting to misbehave in class, too."
>
> For Clara's mother, her daughter's improvement meant that she could relax and enjoy herself a little. Divorced for several years, she began putting more energy into her social life and going out on dates on the weekends. But for Clara, her progress seemed to result in less attention from her mother. Her decline in behavior and grades was unconsciously designed to let her mother know that she still needed extra encouragement. Once she understood the reasons behind Clara's backsliding, her mother was able to reassure her daughter of her continuing support, and Clara's grades and behavior steadily improved.

Sabotaging the Self

Although backsliding may result when parents withdraw support prematurely, by far the greatest threat to the treatment effort arises from the underachiever's own distorted beliefs. Deep down, the underachiever believes that she is a stupid, unlovable person who does not deserve to be successful. As a result, she may unconsciously undermine her own efforts and those of her parents and teachers so that she achieves the negative results she expects.

"Ever since I got an A on my Spanish midterm, my dad's started talking about big-name colleges again," confided Larry, an apprehensive look creeping over his face. "What if I can't keep this up? Suppose I flunk the exam?"

Despite what parents may hope, getting a few good grades does not automatically lead to high self-esteem and continued high achievement for the underachiever. In fact, as we have seen, the underachiever expects any success to be followed by failure. Thus, instead of giving her confidence, improvement leads initially to the fear that some catastrophe is just around the corner—and an abrupt return to her old habits. Moreover, trying hard *in and of itself* is frightening for the underachiever. Because she believes that she is incompetent, she unconsciously fears that persisting will drain her of the few internal resources she possesses and leave her more vulnerable than before.

The underachiever also resists sustaining the effort to change her ways because she fears that everyone around her will discover that she cannot, after all, achieve in school. Secretly she worries that she has low ability and is unable to do the work she has so long avoided and devalued. If she begins trying to do well in all of her classes, inevitably there will be some subjects that come more easily to her and others that are more difficult. Whereas she has been telling herself and everyone else that her poor performance has been due to her lack of effort or lack of interest in her studies, now she fears that others will see it was due to her lack of ability. Far better to be called lazy than stupid, she tells herself. Far better to fail to try than to try and fail.

Moreover, as the underachiever begins to take responsibility for her own learning, she has to abandon her unconscious fantasy of being rescued from her predicament. As she gradually realizes that she is succeeding through her own efforts rather than through luck or some external power, she is simultaneously thrilled and terrified. Learning to be self-directed means that she is capable of being an independent person. Like it or not, she is growing up at last.

RESPONDING CONSTRUCTIVELY TO BACKSLIDING

Mrs. Dowling's voice over the telephone sounded desperate. "I can't understand it," she moaned. "Just when it seemed like Allison was getting on the right track in ninth grade, we get this notice from her earth science teacher saying she didn't turn in a six-weeks' project! We didn't even know she had a project!"

What can parents do when the underachiever seems to be undermining his own success? First, parents should not panic. They need to remind themselves, the child, and the child's teachers that change takes time and that minor setbacks are to be expected rather than dreaded. It may be helpful for parents to keep in mind the image of the infant who toddles away from his mother and, meeting something a little different or surprising, runs back to her as fast as his little legs can carry him to check her reaction to his discovery. Displaying alarm at the underachiever's temporary retreat will only reinforce his old belief that exploration is dangerous. "If my parents get anxious at this setback," he will tell himself, "they must not really believe I can cope successfully with my schoolwork."

Second, when a setback occurs, parents should continue to rely on the constructive communication strategies they have learned to promote the underachiever's development of more positive images of the self and of others. They must give him permission to feel discouraged, angry, or anxious without overreacting or providing unwanted advice in an effort to defend themselves against their own worries. In particular, parents should allow the underachiever to express his fears that he will slip back into his old, self-destructive ways. Although this is not an easy task, when the underachiever is able to express his anxieties about setbacks without fear that his parents will respond with even more anxiety of their own, one missing project or one low grade becomes less frightening. Exploring new worlds and new ways of behaving feels much safer when there's a secure place to return to, a place where all kinds of feelings about the journey can be shared.

Later that evening, Mrs. Dowling found a quiet moment when she could talk to Allison alone. "We got a notice from Mr. Benjamin today about your not turning in a project," she said calmly.

"Mom, don't be mad, but I just couldn't think of anything to do it on. And then I sort of forgot about it," confessed her daughter.

"You know, your dad and I have been so proud of how you've brought your grades up in algebra this semester," Mrs. Dowling replied. "That took a lot of effort. And sometimes when people start working harder, they worry whether they can keep it up."

Allison looked relieved. "I've never worked so hard in my life," she admitted. "It was a whole lot easier when I didn't care about my grades."

Just as important, parents need to convey their unshakable belief that the child will be able to learn from his mistakes and go on to achieve success.

Mrs. Dowling gave her daughter a quick hug. "Allison, I know you're working hard. You've come up two whole grades in math, from an F to a C. That's real progress and your dad and I are proud of you. Next time you have a project, let us know and we'll try to be helpful in any way we can."

"I sure will!" exclaimed Allison, returning the hug. "Thanks for believing in me, Mom!"

SIBLINGS' RESISTANCE TO CHANGE
AND HOW TO COMBAT IT

As the underachiever improves, parents also need to prepare to deal with the negative behaviors his improvement may evoke in his siblings. Parents have often noted with alarm that as the underachiever becomes more successful, a brother or sister begins to show a decline in academic performance, behavior, or both. When there are only two children in the family, the effect is particularly striking:

> *Always a difficult child to manage, Everett had shown signs of underachievement as early as first grade. Now a seven-year-old second grader, he was very restless and inattentive and completed little written work. Although his parents had hoped that he would "grow up" over the summer, he was even more inattentive and unproductive in second grade than he had been in first grade. After several months of counseling with Everett and his parents, his behavior and performance began to improve gradually but steadily.*
>
> *All's well that ends well, right? Wrong. As Everett continued to improve, his five-year-old sister, Nora, became increasingly oppositional. Her behavior and achievement in her kindergarten class deteriorated so much that her parents and teacher were alarmed. Fortunately, her parents realized that Nora was reacting to the loss of her status in the family as the only "good" child and to having to share her parents' approval with her brother. They were able to offer Nora additional support as they continued to encourage Everett, and her school performance returned to its previous high level.*

Although in some families, most or all of the children are underachievers, in the majority of families, there are siblings who are doing much better than the underachiever. Like Nora, these children have in some way benefited from their sibling's underachievement. They have enjoyed being the "smart" child or the "good" child in the family. As the underachiever improves and begins to earn more validation from family members, his siblings may fiercely resist being dislodged from their positions of superiority and criticize the underachiever in an effort to regain their former status. If these efforts to undermine the under-achiever's improvement fail, they may react by underachieving or mis-behaving themselves.

As the underachiever begins the transformation process, therefore, parents should be prepared for other children in the family to react and stand ready to provide both the underachiever and his siblings with ex-tra support. Parents must not tolerate discouragement, teasing, or criti-cism from the underachiever's brothers and sisters. Although parents cannot be present all the time to monitor how siblings treat each other and to protect the underachiever from every negative interaction with his siblings, they can make it clear that the family's job is to support his efforts to change. Moreover, as he feels more secure of his parents' sup-port, he will become more assertive with his siblings, just as he is be-coming more self-directed at school.

TEACHER RESPONSES TO CHANGE

Like parents, teachers have been waiting, sometimes for a long time, for the underachiever to improve. As a result, teachers, like parents, may greet the first signs of change not with praise and delight but with dis-belief or disappointment that improvement has taken so long to arrive. Communications to and about the child that reflect these ambivalent feelings can undermine the underachiever's commitment to change, es-pecially if they are delivered in front of his classmates.

"Sam, it's great that you're completing more homework in English. I just wish you'd done this earlier."

"Alice, is this your homework? Wonders will never cease!"

"Jordan turned in a social studies project on time? I can't believe it! Let me sit down and try to get over the shock!" (Laughter from the rest of the students.)

Such destructive communications can undo the underachiever's first faltering steps toward change. Especially when a teacher's comments about his improvement seem to invite peer ridicule, the child may become so angry that he secretly resolves never to do any work for that teacher again.

HELPING TEACHERS SUPPORT POSITIVE CHANGE

Because teachers wield tremendous influence in the treatment process, parents must help them support positive change by modeling constructive ways of encouraging the child's efforts to improve without dwelling on the past:

> *"Mr. Jarvis, Anthony knows that we wish he'd been working this hard all year, so we try not to remind him about his poor grades last semester. We just focus on letting him know how pleased we are about the positive changes in his performance now."*

Parents can also help teachers support change by asking them to provide regular feedback to the child on her progress. This feedback should be verbal rather than written. That way, if the feedback is positive, the child can report it to the parent. If not, she is under no obligation to do so. Regular teacher feedback that is accurate without being critical reminds the child that her teacher is genuinely interested in her progress and helps counteract the feelings of hopelessness that can plague the underachiever at the beginning of treatment. Adults sometimes fail to realize how much a single encouraging comment from a teacher means to a child, especially to the underachiever who has believed for so long that no one was responsive to her needs.

> *"Mrs. Jackson always stands by the door and whispers to me how I did that day before I go home,"* related Teresa, *a third grader with a long history of misbehavior and poor achievement. "I really like it when she says I've had a good day."* She smiled a beatific smile. *"I'm going to have a good day tomorrow, too!"*

Parents can also help teachers cope with the roller coaster ride of progress by refusing to become discouraged themselves. When parents convey their confidence in the child's ability to change to the teacher as well as to the underachiever herself, the teacher will interpret any setbacks accordingly.

At the end of the school day, Mrs. Bates sat wearily at the back of the room, a stack of ungraded workbooks piled on the reading table. "You know, some days I get so tired of trying to deal with all these kids and all their problems," she confessed. "But I have to tell you, Joshua's parents are so supportive of everything I do and are trying so hard to help him at home that I can't give up on him either. He's having a rough time right now, but he'll pick up again, I'm sure."

WHEN TO SEEK PROFESSIONAL HELP

If the underachiever does not show signs of improvement within a reasonable time despite her parents' best efforts to use the strategies outlined in this book, the parents should seek professional help. This lack of improvement suggests unconscious fears within the underachiever or other family members that any changes in her may threaten the integrity of the family unit. In such cases, it is critical for parents to obtain the services of a qualified mental health professional so that the entire family can receive support throughout the transformation process.

As noted earlier, in some families, the child's underachievement has been serving a vital function in the overall security of the family system. It may be distracting attention from a more catastrophic family problem, such as marital conflict, alcoholism, or the chronic illness of a parent. Because the child's school failure is infinitely less terrifying to her than the fear that her family will break up or her parents will be unable to parent her, she becomes an underachiever to divert attention from what she perceives as a much more serious problem—the dissolution of the family and the loss of the people she most loves and needs.

THERAPY AS A SECURE BASE

When parents seek therapy, it does *not* mean that they are bad parents or that the underachiever is emotionally disturbed. It means that they have recognized they are trapped in a destructive interactional pattern with the child that is painful for everyone and is having negative effects on the child's school progress. Most of all, it means that the parents are committed to helping their child achieve her potential and that they have the courage to seek help in that process.

Parents reading this chapter may be protesting, "But my child is the one who has the problem. Why should *I* go to a therapist?" The approach set forth in this book is based on the premise that underachievement derives from ineffective patterns of parent-child interaction. Thus, treatment involving both parents and child provides the best and fastest results. Just as available, responsive parents serve as a secure base for the child, so a sensitive, empathic therapist can serve as a secure base for parents and underachiever alike. He can provide a safe place where family members can examine their old, ineffective communication patterns and learn new and more rewarding ways of relating to each other.

From this perspective, therapy has three basic goals that parallel the basic strategies for change outlined in the preceding chapters: (1) promoting constructive communication between parents and child; (2) helping parents increase the child's feelings of security and competency at home; and (3) helping parents work with teachers to increase the child's security and competency at school. In addition, therapy can help parents examine their parenting styles and the relationship between the parenting they received in their own families and their present-day dealings with the child. Here the aim is not to blame parents or their families of origin but to increase parents' understanding of how maladaptive interactional patterns can be transmitted from generation to generation—and how to end that destructive cycle once and for all.

FINDING A THERAPIST

How can parents find an appropriate therapist to help the underachiever? Asking school mental health professionals, including the counselor, psychologist, or social worker, for suggestions for therapists is a good way to begin. Involving these individuals in the treatment effort can be helpful in several ways. Not only can they help parents identify appropriate counseling agencies and therapists in the community, they can also be invaluable as school-based supports, providing information on the child's progress to parents and therapists and encouraging teachers throughout the process of change. Other good resources for finding a therapist are the family's physician or pediatrician. In metropolitan areas, many hospitals provide departments of psychiatric and psychological services located within the children's health services center, with a staff specializing in children's learning and behavioral problems. Generally the parents and child are scheduled for a consultation with an intake worker. On the basis of the results of the consultation, referrals for treatment are made either to staff members or to community mental health professionals.

Persons with the title of therapist come from a number of mental health professions, including clinical social workers, counseling psychologists, clinical psychologists, psychiatrists, and marriage and family therapists. Parents should ask whether the individual is licensed in her profession and has a medical degree (M.D.), doctoral degree in psychology (Ph.D. or Psy.D.), doctoral degree in education (Ed.D., Ph.D., or D.A.Ed.), or advanced degree in social work (L.C.S.W. or A.C.S.W.). Parents should inquire about the therapist's training and experience, especially in working with underachievers, and ask for references from other parents or school personnel.

Whenever I talk with parents of an underachiever about therapy, I emphasize that working with a therapist is like working with a dentist. Because the treatment process can be difficult and even painful at times, they need to find someone they can really trust. Parents should look for a therapist who is not only well qualified but able to provide the kind of secure base that the underachiever so desperately needs if she is to try out new ways of thinking and behaving. This means a therapist who listens more than she talks, suggests rather than prescribes, and provides support for parents as well as the underachiever herself. Scheduling consultations with several professionals is advisable before making a final choice.

Forms of Therapy

Among the different forms of therapy that may be offered to the under-achiever and her family are individual therapy, group therapy, parent counseling, or family therapy. Group therapy for underachievers is seldom very helpful, especially when the group is composed entirely of underachievers. It is difficult enough for a therapist to be optimally available and responsive to one underachieving and often resistant youngster, much less six or eight underachievers. Moreover, preadolescent and adolescent boys are likely to spend much of their time in group therapy trying to "outcool" each other and being provocative and disruptive rather than practicing more adaptive ways of coping with their negative feelings.

Because parents are the most powerful agents in the treatment process, therapy should involve them as well as their child, preferably with the same professional who is seeing their child. Some therapists may prefer to treat the family as a unit, seeing the parents and child and perhaps the other siblings as well in the same session. For elementary school underachievers, I prefer working primarily with the parents as a couple and involving the child in sessions less frequently, perhaps once a month. Adolescents require a different treatment approach, however. Because their maladaptive views of themselves and others have had more time to solidify, a combination of individual therapy for the child and counseling for the parents is needed. Moreover, it can be very difficult for adolescent underachievers to admit in front of their parents that they need help in changing their attitudes and behaviors. Having some time alone with the therapist can help them feel secure enough to acknowledge that they have a problem and to invest in the treatment process.

To maximize treatment efforts, regular consultation among parents, teachers, and therapist is essential. Parents should sign a permission form for the therapist to consult with the child's teachers and school counselor. Such agreements can be time-limited and extend only for a semester or school year. In addition, parents should request that the therapist attend periodic school meetings to discuss the child's progress with her teachers and reevaluate and refine intervention strategies, if necessary.

Parental Fears About Entering Therapy

The idea of seeing a therapist can feel very threatening to the parents of an underachiever. They may worry, "Will the therapist point out all the things I've been doing wrong all these years? Suppose the therapist says it's too late for my child to be helped?" Therapy is not intended to blame parents. Rather, it offers parents the opportunity to explore their feelings about being parents and their efforts to help their child without fear of criticism. Nor should parents worry that the underachiever will love them less if he forms a relationship with a therapist. On the contrary, with a safe place to express his fears of disappointing himself and his parents, he will be more able to demonstrate his love for his family and channel his energies in positive directions.

For their part, having the secure base of therapy can help parents come to terms with old, painful memories that they have long labored to repress but that have been reactivated by their child's school experiences. Like the underachiever, all of us often try to avoid our painful feelings by repressing our needs, withdrawing from challenges, or sabotaging our own successes. The process of helping the underachiever can serve as an opportunity for all family members to reflect on their methods of coping with the stresses and obstacles of everyday life and the way in which they interact with each other. It can especially be an opportunity for parents to strengthen and enrich their own relationship, which has often been neglected in their struggle to deal with the underachiever and his problems.

The Underachiever's Fears About Entering Therapy

"What do you mean I have to go talk to some counselor?" exclaimed Milo. "There's nothing wrong with me! I'm not crazy!"

"But he doesn't want to go to a therapist," parents may be saying. Indeed, most underachievers initially claim that they don't want to talk to anyone about their problems. (They don't have any problems, remember?) Just as underachievers find it difficult to accept help from their parents and teachers, so they are likely to find it hard at first to accept help from a therapist and to talk openly about their feelings of inadequacy and fear of failure. For these reasons, underachievers, especially adolescents, may resist going to therapy and, once there, may try to avoid talking about anything meaningful for the first few sessions.

To encourage the underachiever's investment in this part of treatment, parents should present the idea of therapy as a support for the whole family rather than a treatment to "fix" the underachiever. The message of this approach is that the parents care so much about helping the child that not only are they willing to take him to a therapist, they are willing to go themselves. In two-parent households, going to therapy should be presented as a decision that *both* parents have made.

> *"Nathan, your mother and I have talked it over, and we want very much to do everything we can to help you be happier and more successful at school. We've scheduled a meeting with Dr. Rathvon next Wednesday at five o'clock to talk about ways we can work as a family to help that happen. She says she'll talk to us for a while and then she'll talk to you about how you see things. We're really looking forward to learning how we can be more helpful to you."*

Although parents may worry that the underachiever may resist therapy, their fears are usually exaggerated. The underachiever knows that he is unsuccessful, feels bad about it, and will often seek help on his own if he is given the opportunity.

> *"Excuse me, are you the lady who talks to kids who have problems? Do you have any time to talk to me?" The plaintive voice came from inside the principal's office. Looking in, I found a small boy sitting dejectedly in a chair. A whispered conversation with the principal revealed that the youngster had been sent to take a timeout in the office for refusing to do his work and causing a disturbance in his fourth-grade class.*

THE CONTINUING NEED FOR A SECURE BASE

"You know, it's not so hard to talk about bad things if you have company." (seven-year-old underachieving boy at the end of a therapy session)

The need for a secure base does not end with childhood. In fact, our need for reliable and responsive attachment figures increases as we grow older and are forced to contemplate the fact of our own mortality and the realization that not all of our hopes and dreams have been fulfilled. If parents are to help the underachiever realize his full potential and attain their own potential in their multiple roles as parent, wage-earner, homemaker, and spouse, they will need to find support for themselves as well.

Parents can begin to examine their own support system by asking, "What kinds of things do I do that make me feel good about myself? What activities do I engage in that make me feel valued and competent?" Today's parents are pulled in so many directions that they are often in a chronic state of physical and mental exhaustion and have little time to pursue their own interests and pleasures. No parents who are constantly feeling depleted and unappreciated can be expected to provide the kind of security and validation that children need, however good their intentions.

Even more important, the parents of an underachiever need to build a supportive network of people. All of us need a sanctuary—somewhere to share the good times and take refuge from the bad. In the case of the underachiever, packed full of potential but resisting all efforts to get it out of him, his parents need reliable supports for themselves so they can try out new, more constructive ways of communicating with him that offer him the opportunity to change.

SOLVING THE MYSTERY OF UNDERACHIEVEMENT

Solving the mystery of underachievement means change for both parents and child. Although the younger the individual, the easier it is for him to change, change is possible at all ages, and all family members can learn to direct their development along more rewarding pathways. Although parents cannot begin again in raising their children or go back to alter their relationships with their own parents, they can recognize and modify their own interactional patterns with the child that have been unwittingly inhibiting his achievement.

To solve the mystery of their child's underachievement, parents must abandon the hope that they can try to make *him* change. Instead, with a new understanding of his distorted internal world and of external factors that perpetuate his maladaptive views of himself and those around him, parents can change the way in which *they* interact with him. With this approach to treatment, which differs radically from conventional methods for treating underachievers, the child's sense of security and his motivation for learning are immeasurably enhanced. In and of itself, his parents' commitment to understanding *his* point of view and helping him chart his own pathway toward achievement increases his self-esteem and his ability to persist with difficult tasks, including the most difficult task of all—growing up.

After all, the genuine achiever is defined not only by his excellent performance but also by his love of learning for learning's sake. By communicating their belief in their child's fundamental worth and competency, parents can help him to achieve—and to *want* to achieve. Such a child is able not merely to achieve the tasks that others set for him but to develop his own goals and to work happily and diligently to attain them. Solving the mystery of their child's underachievement is one of the most demanding tasks parents will ever undertake, but the rewards are great—for the child, for the family, and for society as a whole.

Recommended Reading

Bettelheim, Bruno. 1988. *A good-enough parent: A book on child rearing*. New York: Vintage Books.

In this refreshing alternative to "how-to" parenting books, the great psychotherapist and humanist proposes that mistakes in child rearing arise from the intensity of the parent-child bond and guides parents in facilitating development in terms of the child's needs and interests rather than their own.

Bettelheim, Bruno. 1970. *Surviving and other essays*. New York: Alfred A. Knopf.

Collection of moving essays on topics ranging from adolescence to the Holocaust. The second section, on education, includes the insightful essay "The decision to fail," which describes how parents can help children overcome emotional blocks to school success.

Bettelheim, Bruno. 1976. *The uses of enchantment: The meaning and importance of fairy tales*. New York: Alfred A. Knopf.

A fascinating account of the significance of fairy tales and their value in helping children understand and resolve life's conflicts. Illuminates the nature of the psychological tasks every person must master to achieve autonomy.

Bowlby, John. 1982. *Attachment and loss, Vol 1. Attachment* (2d ed.). New York: Basic Books.

Bowlby, John. 1973. *Attachment and loss, Vol 2. Separation: Anxiety and anger*. New York: Basic Books.

Bowlby, John. 1980. *Attachment and loss, Vol 3. Loss: Sadness and depression*. New York: Basic Books.

These three volumes make up Bowlby's monumental trilogy on intimate relationships and the consequences of their disruption for a person's functioning and future relationships. Contains a wealth of insights for parents and anyone involved in caring for children.

Bowlby, John. 1979. *The making and breaking of affectional bonds*. New York: Tavistock Publications.

Collection of lectures chronicling the effects on emotional development of the formation and disruption of close relationships. The essay "Self-reliance and some conditions that promote it" is especially useful for parents wishing to encourage responsibility in their children.

Bowlby, John. 1989. *A secure base: Parent-child attachment and healthy human development*. New York: Basic Books.

Series of lectures by the founder of attachment theory on the role of parent-child interactions in personality development and the need of all human beings for secure, supportive relationships.

Ginott, Haim. 1965. *Between parent and child*. New York: Avon.

Classic work by a prominent child psychotherapist on how parents can help children develop self-esteem and self-motivation. Illustrated with many examples of the differences between helpful and unhelpful parent-child communication.

Ginott, Haim. 1975. *Between teacher and child: A book for parents and teachers*. New York: Avon.

Written for both parents and teachers, this compassionate and useful book offers a wealth of practical suggestions for helping children become happy and productive students.

Stern, Daniel 1985. *The interpersonal world of the infant: A view from psychoanalysis and developmental psychology*. New York: Basic Books.

Complex but important work by a psychoanalyst and infant researcher tracing the emergence of the infant as an emotional being. Stern's theory of how parents' own emotional experiences shape their child's feelings and behavior has profound implications for both parenting and teaching.

Index

drug abuse, 30, 34
dumb, as term of devaluation, 131–32

eating disorders, 90
educational choices, 32, 33, 34, 39
    restriction of, 36–37
educational evaluation, 69
Education for All Handicapped Children
    Act (Public Law 94–142), 47–48
effective questions, 184–88
    encouragement of, 187–88
    ineffective vs., 185–87, 188
elementary school, 41, 82–84, 100,
    154, 162, 198, 224
    developmental immaturity explana-
        tions in, 39–40, 50
    disorganization in, 68
    grading policies in, 41, 57
    homework time for, 155
    independent effort in, 78
    individual progress report in, 109
    parental participation in life at,
        193–94
    reading levels in, 56
    report cards in, 41, 56
    retention in, 112
    seating arrangements in, 176
    warning signs in, 23–26
emotional disturbances (ED), 60, 61
    as cause of misbehavior, 210
empathy, 127–28, 171, 187
entitlement, sense of, 79, 112
expectations, fulfillment of, *see* nega-
    tive outcomes; negative responses,
    evocation of
exploration, independent, 66, 70, 75,
    81, 86, 93, 94, 95, 97, 216
extracurricular activities, 156

family system, 221
    siblings in, 218–19, 224
family therapy, 224
fantasies, 82–84
    grandiose, 37
    of magical rebirth, 75
    of magical rescue, 71–73, 75–76

of superiority, 77, 79
fathers, 149–50, 193, 194
fine motor coordination disabilities, 48
fire setting, 210
food additives, 42, 50
Freud, Sigmund, 7, 13

gazing-into-space behavior, 72, 92–93
gifted students, 22
    boredom of, 15, 46–47, 113, 114
gloomy predictions, 126, 141
goal setting, perfectionistic, 77–78,
    114–15, 132
golden age of achievement, 82–84
grades, 24, 30, 39, 40, 75, 114–15, 213
    classroom seating position linked to,
        176
    entitlement to, 79
    lack of control over, 67
    warning notices concerning, 70
grading policies, 41, 56–57
gross motor coordination disabilities,
    48–49
group therapy, 224
growing up, ambivalence about, 75–76,
    80–84, 148
    golden age of achievement and,
        82–84
    regressive behavior in, 80–82
guidance counselors, high school,
    32–33
"hall buddy," 198
help, 24, 70–76, 80, 81, 86, 92, 93, 122,
    127, 170
    asking for, 57, 74, 96–101, 141,
        158–60, 184
    coming too late, 74–75
    fantasies of, 71–73, 75–76
    misinterpretation of, 73–74
    wrong kind of, 75–76
helplessness:
    affirmation of, 129–30
    overcome by helping others,
        200–201
helpless questions, 185–87
"help sessions," after-school, 179

About the Author

After sixteen years of working with parents and children as a teacher, elementary school counselor, and middle school guidance director, Natalie Rathvon is currently a psychologist and educational consultant in private practice in Maryland. She holds two doctorates, a Ph.D. in clinical psychology from George Washington University and a Ph.D. in education from George Mason University. She is a licensed Psychologist in the District of Columbia and Maryland and a licensed Professional Counselor in Virginia. She has served as an adjunct professor at George Mason University, a guest lecturer at George Washington University, and an editorial board member of *Elementary School Guidance & Counseling*. Currently she is consultant to several schools and community agencies on projects ranging from training new teachers to accommodating diverse learners in the regular classroom. She has published many articles in education and counseling journals and frequently conducts workshops for parents, teachers, and mental health professionals on a wide variety of topics, including psychological testing, classroom management, and encouraging school success.